The Whale Watchers' Guide

Robert Gardner

illustrated by Don Sineti

Julian Messner  New York

Published by Julian Messner,
A Division of Simon & Schuster, Inc.
Simon & Schuster Building,
1230 Avenue of the Americas,
New York, New York 10020

JULIAN MESSNER and colophon are trademarks of
Simon & Schuster, Inc.

Manufactured in the United States of America

Design by Howard Petlack, A Good Thing, Inc.

Library of Congress Cataloging in Publication Data

Gardner, Robert, 1929–
    The whale watchers' guide.

    Bibliography: p.
    Includes index.
    Summary: Discusses whales and whaling and explains how
to tell one whale from another and how to watch them
from land and sea.
    1. Whales—Juvenile literature. 2. Wildlife watching
—Juvenile literature. [1. Whales. 2. Wildlife watching]
I. Sineti, Don.   II. Title.
QL737.C4G235   1984   599.5   83-17425

ISBN: 0-671-45811-6
       0-671-49807-X Pbk.

10 9 8 7 6 5 4 3 2

Other Books by Robert Gardner

Kitchen Chemistry
Save That Energy
Water: The Life Sustaining Resource

Contents

A Note on the Illustrations

The drawings in this book have been prepared especially to show what whales actually look like out on the open water. In the drawings the parts of the whale's body above the surface of the water are darker than the parts below the surface. In the identification profiles the parts of the whale's body appear in the sequence they are most likely to be seen on the water: blow (spout), back, and tail.

Whale Watching

"And God created great whales"

From the Whale Overlook near Cabrillo National Monument at the tip of Point Loma near San Diego, California, to the coastal waters near the Pilgrims' Monument in Provincetown, Massachusetts, whales have captured the eyes and hearts of Americans. Whale watching has become a favorite pastime and has blossomed into a multi-million-dollar business that continues to grow along both coasts.

Watching Whales from Land

For landlubbers, whale watching is difficult, but it can be done. A pair of binoculars or a telescope will improve the viewing. The best locations for this activity are along the West Coast. Promontories such as Point Loma near San Diego, Point Dume, Point Vicente, Point La Jolla, Cabrillo Beach, Cape Lookout in Oregon, Cascade Head, Marine Museum in San Pedro near Point Fermin, Dana Point, South Coast Bluffs, and the mouth of Wickaninish Bay in British Columbia, which is visible from Pacific Rim National Park's Box Island all provide a clear view of coastal waters.

The best time to see gray whales from Point Loma is during the winter when these gray giants of the sea migrate southward to Baja California. A five-hour ferry and auto ride from Vancouver in March or April will enable you to watch the gray whales as they "march" northward toward Alaska and their summer feeding seas.

A much longer trip is necessary to watch gray whales from the piers where salt used to be loaded on ships in Laguna Guerro Negro near Scammond's Lagoon in Baja. The piers make ideal platforms for watching the whales that swim by only a few feet away. With patience and luck, you might observe whales from the shores of Cape Cod, too, but, with boats beckoning visitors to take a better look, few would pass up the chance to get a closer view of whales on a half-day whale-watching cruise.

Watching Whales on Short Cruises

A two- to eight-hour boat ride can bring you very close to whales. Dramamine and a stable position near the center rear of the boat will prevent you from succumbing to motion sickness. Queasiness may pass as the excitement of seeing whales takes over. One of my shipmates on a recent whale-watching cruise aboard the *Ranger III* out of Provincetown, Massachusetts, felt the pangs of motion sickness on the outbound voyage, when seas were calm, but was fine on the trip home, despite a squall and seas that were very rough.

People along the West Coast can approach gray whales at sea from excursion boats out of San Diego, Oceanside, Dana Point, Newport Beach, Redondo Beach, Marina Del Ray, Long Beach, San Pedro, Santa Monica, Ventura, Santa Barbara, Avila, Monterey, Santa Cruz, Half Moon Bay, San Francisco, Bodega, and Puget Sound where killer whales as well as grays are seen frequently.

At the piers in Provincetown, Massachusetts, you will find boats that carry whale watchers to the waters of Cape Cod Bay and beyond. Similar tours originate from Plymouth and from Barnstable Harbor on Cape Cod in Massachusetts, Montauk Point at the eastern end of Long Island, New York; New Haven, Connecticut; Hampton Beach, New Hampshire, and numerous other places along the Atlantic coast, particularly from Atlantic City, New Jersey, to the coast of Maine and northward to Newfoundland and the mouth of the St. Lawrence River.

These four- to eight-hour cruises will provide views of fin whales, humpbacks, Minke whales, dolphins, porpoises, and occasionally a right whale, a beluga, a pilot whale, and killer whales.

For those interested in the history of whaling, the whaling museums in Sharon, Nantucket, and New Bedford, Massachusetts, and Mystic, Connecticut, are all within a few hours' travel by car or boat from New York or Boston.

Those who live in, or travel to, Alaska or Hawaii can find whale-watching cruises that leave from the shores of these two states as well. The Kapalua Bay Hotel in West Maui uses its own catamaran to provide hour-long whale-watching sails for guests. Details about current whale-watching cruises in Hawaii can be obtained from the Pacific Whale Foundation, Kihei, Hawaii 96753.

The *Dolphin* Fleet out of Provincetown is operated by Captain Albert Avellar, a former charter fishing boat captain who pioneered whale watching back in 1975. In those days people didn't believe there were whales in Cape Cod Bay. He had to assure the first groups he took on board that he would refund their money if no whales were sighted. This promise really wasn't much of a risk because Avellar and all Cape Cod fishermen knew the whales were there, and they knew roughly where to find them.

Today, from spring until late fall, *Dolphin III* and *Dolphin IV* make whale-watching trips every day of the week.

At first, Captain Avellar tried to attract whales closer to his boat by broadcasting music on loudspeakers, but he soon learned that as the whales came to know the ships, only kindness was needed. Though fin whales remain shy about approaching ships, humpbacks will usually put on a good show. They often breach (leap from and fall back into the water), stunning fish, which gulls then swoop in to eat. Or the humpbacks may spy-hop ("stand" vertically in the water with head above water), wave their flippers, and swim near or even under the boat. It's not unusual to see a humpback's tail above water to port and its head visible to starboard.

The *Dolphin* Fleet has on board for each trip a naturalist such as David Mattila or Dr. Charles "Stormy" Mayo of the Cetacean Research Program at the Center for Coastal Studies. (Whales, porpoises, and dolphins belong to the scientific order Cetacea.) The naturalists, who are collecting data for their research, provide the 75,000 whale-watching enthusiasts who make the voyage each year with information about whales.

We boarded the *Dolphin IV*, the faster of the two ships of this fleet, one bright, crisp morning in late August. We were sipping coffee purchased on board shortly after 8:00 A.M. as we enjoyed a beautiful view of the harbor and the monument that projects well above the old buildings of Provincetown. Flags were flapping in the breeze, gulls flew overhead, and early morning fishing boats were returning to port.

It was a peaceful, pleasant setting, broken only by the cries of children, probably too young to enjoy such a voyage, and the reprimands of their parents who only now, after paying $10 for each child and $12 for themselves, realized they might have made a mistake.

An older child wondered, "What are those funny noises?"

The noises were whale sounds that had been recorded and were being played for the enjoyment of the passengers.

At 8:30 A.M., Stormy Mayo, the naturalist for the trip, gave a short lecture on whale watching and explained the nature of the scientific mission we were about to undertake.

His talk was informative but couched in terms that some found difficult to follow, since they were not students of cetology, the study of whales.

His final words were that the trip would be rough because of the winds and that we might not be able to get far enough north to see the humpbacks that were beginning to move back into the waters off Cape Cod. He recommended Dramamine for those who were concerned about seasickness.

Fortunately, most passengers took his advice, for the seas were indeed high and the trip was rough for the first two hours.

As we cruised out of the harbor, Dr. Mayo was at the bow to point out our course on a chart, but there was room for only a dozen or so of the hundred or more on board to see the chart and ask questions of this competent scientist.

It became clear that we would not be able to cruise far enough north to see humpbacks, so the captain spent about three hours pursuing the spouts of fin whales. While we were unable, at first, to get very close to the elusive fin whales, Dr. Mayo was later able to photograph the chevrons on the backs of several of these whales. For purposes of standardizing sightings and identifying the whales, the photographs are taken from the whale's right side so observers see the fin whale's white lower jaw. Its left jaw is dark. (See Chapter 2.)

At about 11:15 A.M. we came upon a cow and calf and were able to follow them over the course of three lengthy surfacings. The captain kept the boat parallel and close to the whales' path, providing an excellent view of these animals as they moved through the water leaving their "footprints" behind.

We got several more, less impressive views of fin whales before we headed back from the waters east of Provincetown shortly after noon at higher speeds and on calmer seas.

We had logged seven different fin whales during our five-hour trip, but were unable to observe any other species on this particular day.

Whale watchers turned their faces sunward and many dozed as we rounded Race Point and "steamed" for port. Few were disappointed, though some said they would opt for calmer seas on their next whale watch.

On Board the Ranger III

A trip aboard the *Ranger III* is similar to one on the *Dolphin*, but there are differences. The *Ranger* is a slower boat, and the cruise is four hours instead of five. The reduced range due to speed and time means that this boat is unable to search for whales as far from shore as the *Dolphin* fleet.

The *Ranger* captains are able to provide whale watchers with excellent close-up views of whales, and naturalist Steve Morello is informative, helpful, and entertaining. The crew aboard the *Ranger* provides a less scientific voyage than do the members of the *Dolphin* fleet. On the *Ranger* they are less involved in collecting data and more concerned, I felt, in giving their passengers a good look at whales.

Steve's approach as a naturalist is informal. He avoids the use of scientific names for the whales, and sprinkles humor throughout his lectures. There was also a greater opportunity to ask questions aboard the *Ranger*, and laughter flowed freely.

For those with a scientific bent, the *Dolphin* fleet is probably the correct choice. Those who enjoy a less scientific, more informal approach to whale watching will find the *Ranger* to their liking.

To illustrate the *Ranger's* attempt to entertain as well as to find whales, Paul Winter of the Paul Winter Consort played on each of four whale-watching cruises on September 13 and 14, 1982. In addition, Winter conducted two workshops on music with animal sounds in the Provincetown Town Hall.

These are but two of the styles you will find aboard whale-watching boats. Each boat and, in fact, each voyage, is unique. If you are fortunate enough to be able to choose from among several whale-watching cruises, obtain information about each. If possible, talk to people who have gone on the whale watch you contemplate taking before you go on board. Decide if it's the right cruise for you. But don't expect miracles. Whales do move around, and whale-watching ships can only *look* for whales. They don't know exactly where to find them. You might be lucky and go on a day when dolphins are in the area or when orcas pass through, or even find a migrating right whale in the spring or fall. You may see humpbacks frolicking in a pool, feeding, breaching, or spy-hopping. You might see a finback in a rare breach, or a minke whale feeding. On the other hand, although it's rare not to see a single whale, it does happen. If it should happen to you, you'll probably get a rain check. If you do, use it! It's worth a second trip, or more, to see these amazing mammals.

Growing interest in whales has led to an increasing number of whale-watching trips along both American coasts. If you live near the coast, chances are you can find whale-watching cruises not far from your home. Check the Yellow Pages of your telephone book and the amusement section of your newspaper, as well as the advertisements; or call a travel agency or boating firm. Don't be discouraged if you can't find "whale watching" in the yellow pages. Try looking under "boating," "fishing," "cruises," and so forth. Whale watching boats are generally owned by former fishermen who still make occasional fishing trips, too.

The competition among whale-watching boats is sometimes fierce, but the industry is growing so rapidly that no one seems to have difficulty making a go of it.

When you reach the pier where your whale-watching boat is docked, it may be warm, even hot. But out on the water a cool breeze and ocean spray may lower the temperature and increase the windchill factor, so be prepared. Take a sweater or jacket. If rain is likely, take your rain gear. Whales spout in rain or shine.

If you are responsible for young children on the boat, watch them carefully. The vessels have rails, but there is often plenty of space between the rails, and the decks are often slippery when wet. Youngsters should certainly remain inside or below deck if the ship encounters rough seas.

A Week of Whale Watching

For those who enjoy longer trips and cruises, World Wide Divers of New York City provides a chance to get very close to whales with its scuba diving expeditions to the Caribbean.

Week-long cruises by H and M Landing of San Diego will take you to San Ignacio Lagoon on Mexico's Baja California peninsula where, like Steve Swartz, you may learn to identify gray whales by their markings.

Swartz, who was a marine biologist for the San Diego Natural History Museum, which conducts numerous trips to the Baja area, found 245 cows with their calves in San Ignacio Lagoon during the first two weeks of one winter calving season. By the fifth week, there were 450 cows with calves and 110 other whales. Patches of white on their skin, scars, deformities, barnacle growths, and differences in dorsal ridges enabled Swartz to identify individual whales. Such features prove useful in establishing migration routes, learning how much time the whales spend in the lagoon, and determining whether whales return to the same region each year to calve or breed.

In the lagoon you will find "friendly" whales who may blow bubbles beneath your small boat, lift it gently with their tails, and enjoy having their heads patted. Even cows with new calves may grow friendly with time—but, a word of caution: don't get your boat between a cow and her calf.

9

For some unknown reason, gray whales are attracted by the sound of boat engines—a negative adaptation for survival with present whaling methods. They seem to express their "joy" by blowing bubbles near a running engine. When the engine is turned off, they often depart.

Baja Byways and Baja Expeditions, Incorporated, provide air and overland trips to Baja where boats bring you into the 80 square miles of Magdalena Bay, 600 miles below the California–Mexico border. There gray whales abound in the winter and early spring. You will see them spy-hopping, as they turn full circle, or lying lazily in the sun. You might see a calf 15-feet long, and weighing half a ton, feasting on a few of the 50 gallons of fat rich milk that its 50-foot, 35-ton mother provides each day. Perhaps, if you arrive early in the season, before the bulls begin their return trip up the coast to Alaska, you will witness the courtship and unique mating behavior of these gentle gray giants.

A very enjoyable way to cruise and watch whales in cooler waters is on board one of the summertime cruise ships out of Vancouver, Seattle, and some Alaskan ports. These ships enter the fjords of British Columbia where grays and humpbacks are found.

Whales in Aquariums

The best close-range whale viewing you can find is at an aquarium. The whale may stare at you, swim within inches of your eyes, and turn about in all directions providing a view of its entire body. Unfortunately, except on very rare occasions, the only whales you will see there are small-toothed whales such as dolphins or belugas. Aquariums cannot afford to house and feed a large whale for very long.

On the other hand, an aquarium will provide you with an opportunity to see other sea mammals such as the carnivorous seals and sea lions as well as sharks and exotic fish.

Should We Watch Whales?

Whale watching has increased America's interest in and concern for whales. But many conservationists and cetologists fear the effects of whale watching on whales. They claim that the motor sounds of ships entering the inlets of British Columbia frighten away the fish and crustaceans on which whales feed.

Certainly, the "dive bombing" tactics used by some in viewing humpbacks in Hawaiian waters may not be conducive to the courtship, mating, calving, singing, or peace of mind of these animals. The technique used is to rush toward a pod of humpbacks with a speedboat. As the boat gets close to the whales, the driver turns back the motor, and the whale watchers, with their scuba diving equipment, leap into the water in an effort to get an underwater view of the whales.

Similarly, hydrofoils, which are used to view whales off Hawaii and the West Coast, not only stop a humpback in the middle of its song but have had at least two collisions with gray whales off the coast of San Diego.

Others believe the abundance of whale watchers along the California coast has caused the gray whales to move their migration route westward into deeper water. The effects of this change, if any, are difficult to assess.

Are the whales near Baja and elsewhere getting too much love? The whales often seem to enjoy watching humans as much as humans enjoy watching them. But are they ignoring their own reproductive activities because of their interest in "human watching"?

What effect does it have on a whale to be chased by boats? Humpbacks and grays, generally speaking, seem not to mind boats and are often attracted to them. Other species, such as fin whales, avoid boats. And, despite claims to the contrary, many whale-watching boats *do* chase whales. After all, the people on board paid to see whales.

The competitiveness of whale watching is sometimes clearly evident when two boats race to reach the same whale. On the other hand, boats often communicate with one another in locating whales. As more and more fishing vessels get into the whale-watching business, it is likely that regulations will have to be established to govern the conduct of whale-watching boats competing for the "right" to observe the same whale or pod of whales.

While the growth of whale watching may lead to increased competition among boat owners, it also provides increasing opportunities for the public to learn about whales and conservation, and enables scientists to collect more data and find out more about the adaptation, physiology, migration, and behavior patterns of these marvelous mammals.

2

What Is a Whale and How Can I Tell One from Another?

"Suddenly a mighty mass emerged from the water and shot up perpendicularly into the air. It was the whale."

Whales are mammals that live in the sea. Like all mammals, they breathe air, pump their blood with a four chambered heart, and bear their young alive; the females have mammary glands that produce milk for their infant offspring.

Whales are often mistaken for fish because they have lost or internalized all body parts that might impede easy movement through water. Although their forelimbs have become modified into flippers, they still have the same bones found in human arms; their hindlimbs consist only of vestigial bones deep within their bodies; their mammary glands and genitals are enclosed and can be extended to the outside only through narrow mammary or genital slits; and they have no external ears or hair. Whales have no sweat glands to cool their bodies. In fact, they develop a thick layer of fatty blubber beneath their smooth skin. The bones of a whale's skull have been modified to form huge upper

The two blowholes on top of a humpback's head are often visible from a whale-watching vessel.

14

and lower jaws and mouth. Their nostrils, called blowholes, are at the top of the head. The whale breathes through its blowhole. Since whales breathe air, they must surface periodically to exhale old air and inhale fresh oxygen-rich air.

Many whales have a dorsal fin (on the back) to aid their balance; all have a tail with horizontal flukes as opposed to the vertical tail fins of a fish.

Biologists divide all vertebrates (animals with backbones) into classes. These include osteichthyes (bony fish), amphibians, reptiles, aves (birds), and mammals. Within the class Mammalia, animals are grouped into orders such as carnivores, rodents, marsupials, primates, and cetaceans. All whales are cetaceans.

Cetaceans, in turn, are divided into two suborders: Mysticeti and Odontoceti. Odontoceti are the sixty-six or more species of toothed whales, which have from 1 to 260 teeth. There are only ten species within the suborder Mysticeti—the baleen whales. They have no teeth, but the comblike keratin

plates (baleen) that hang from their palates are used to strain out small crustaceans and fish from the water that passes through their mouths.

With a few keys you can probably identify the common whales that live in the coastal waters of North America. A whale can be difficult to identify because so much of its body is submerged, but often a glimpse of some characteristic feature is all you need.

If you find a beached whale, identification is much easier, but you should immediately report your findings to one of the following: (1) National Marine Fisheries Service, 617-281-3600 (Northeast), 813-893-3141 (Southeast), 206-527-6150 (Northwest), 213-548-2575 (Southwest); (2) a marine rescue organization such as the California Marine Mammal Center at the Golden Gate National Recreation Area; (3) a marine park aquarium; (4) your local coast guard station; (5) your local police; (6) the biology department of a nearby university; (7) a humane society.

Keys to Identifying Whales

The following are some details to look for as you observe whales. They will help you to identify the various species described in the next section.

- Does the whale have a dorsal fin?

- If it does, what are its shape, size, and position on the back?

- How long is the whale? If you are on a ship, knowing the ship's length will help you estimate the animal's length.

- Look carefully at the tail flukes. Some species always raise their tails before sounding (diving).

- Does the whale have markings? A pattern? Barnacles?

- What color is the whale? Is one side of its head light and the other side dark?

- What is the shape and height of the whale's spout or blow when it exhales? How much time elapses between blows and during a dive? How many blows occur between dives? Does the dorsal fin appear when the whale blows?

- How large is the whale's head in comparison with its body?

- If it opens its mouth, can you see teeth or baleen?

- Does the whale approach, ignore, or avoid your ship? Does it try to ride the bow wave? Does it react to the stern's wake?

- Does the whale breach (jump out of the water)? If so, does it spin, turn, or somersault?

- Does it spy-hop (stick its head upright out of the water)?

- Is more than one species of whales present?

These details will be useful in identifying the whales in the following list. The list includes only those whales that are reasonably common in the coastal or near coastal waters of North America. A more extensive list with detailed information about each whale can be found in Watson's *Sea Guide to Whales of the World*, which appears in the bibliography.

On most whale-watching trips you will be told what species of whales you are most likely to see. On your way to the whales you can study the material about those species. Some whales are elusive, and you may get only a glimpse of them. To aid in identification you will find in this chapter detailed descriptions of the most common species of whales. Opposite the full length drawing of each whale is a profile chart of the most frequently seen parts of the whale, the blow, back, and tail, in sequence, as they are likely to appear on the open water.

The Baleen Whales: Suborder Mysticeti

The Latin word "Mysticeti" comes from the Greek "mysticetes" which means, "mustached whales." The "mustache," which is really the fringed baleen that hangs from these whales' palates, is visible only when the animals open their mouths.

Eight of the ten species of baleen whales are included in this chapter. They range in size from the 30-foot minke whale to the blue whale, the largest animal that has ever lived on earth.

The common name for each whale is given, followed by its scientific name, genus, and species, in parentheses.

The Right Whale

(Balaena glacialis)

The right whale (*Balaena glacialis*) was given its name by early whalers who considered this the "right" whale to catch because it is slow and floats when dead. The average length of a right whale is 50 feet, and it weighs about 100 tons. There is *no dorsal fin* on its smooth back.

A "bonnet," which is really a series of lumps or callosities (horny growths) infested with barnacles, worms, and lice, sits atop its head in front of its two blowholes through which it emits a double V-shaped spout. Because its blowholes are far apart the blow consists of two distinct spouts that rise as high as 16 feet. Callosities also give each animal a characteristic mustache, goatee, and sideburns on its black skin, which is usually marked by irregular white patches around its chin and navel.

Its huge lower jaw hides the gray or yellowish baleen that may be seen if the whale is feeding.

Right whales are quite rare but may be found in shallow coastal waters off Newfoundland and Alaska, though they do migrate southward in the winter.

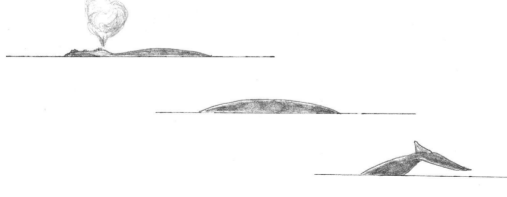

The Bowhead Whale

(Balaena mysticetus)

The bowhead whale (*Balaena mysticetus*), or the Greenland right whale, resembles the right whale, but its head is huge, often one-third the length of its body. It inhabits only Arctic waters and can be distinguished from the right whale by the white bib beneath its chin.

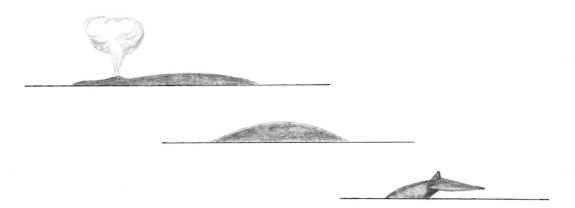

The Gray Whale

(Eschrichtius robustus)

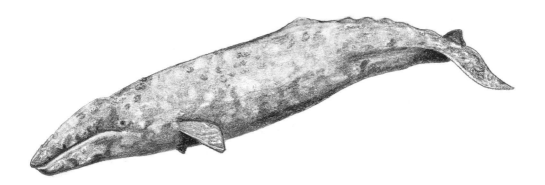

The gray whale (*Eschrichtius robustus*) is 40 to 50 feet long. The weight of an average female is 38 tons (male, about 28 tons). The gray has no dorsal fin, but it does have a hump followed by a series of seven to fifteen bumps along the lower back. The spout is usually a single column.

The mottled gray skin with patches of white barnacles distinguishes the gray from all other whales.

Gray whales are found in the shallow western coastal waters of the United States in the winter, and in the lagoons of the Baja peninsula during the winter and early spring.

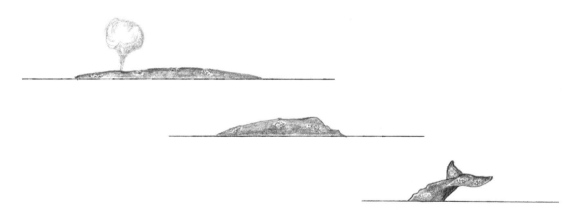

The Fin Whale

(Balaenoptera physalus)

The fin whale (*Balaenoptera physalus*) like all the rorquals (fin, blue, Minke, sei, Bryde's, and humpback) has grooves in the flesh beneath its lower jaws and throat.

Fin whales are second only to blue whales in size. Their average length is 70 feet for males and 82 feet for females. They weigh 40 to 50 tons and are the fastest large whales. They have small flippers and a short dorsal fin located two-thirds of the way between snout and tail.

Their upper bodies are dark gray or umber while their ventral sides (undersides) are light. The head is unique. The left side is dark, but the right lower jaw, baleen, and tongue are relatively unpigmented and so appear white as they emerge from the sea.

When a fin whale surfaces, it blows a single tall (12–20 feet) spray that widens at the top. Slowly it rolls its back and dorsal fin above the water. This motion is repeated four or five times at ten- to twenty-second intervals. In the last roll, the back rises more steeply prior to the whale's five- to fifteen-minute sounding.

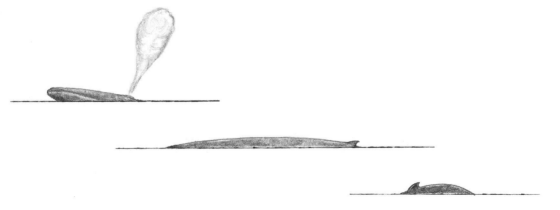

The Blue Whale

(Balaena musculus)

The blue whale (*Balaena musculus*) is the largest animal ever to exist. The male may average 82 feet in length, and the female, 102 feet. A rare blue may weigh as much as 200 tons after a summer feeding, but the average is about 120 tons.

This long, graceful, streamlined whale stays in the open ocean, migrating from polar to tropical waters. Its color is marine blue-gray, though in polar waters it often becomes coated with yellow-green algae; hence, the nickname, sulfur bottom.

Several shallow dives at about twenty-second intervals are followed by a sounding that may last half an hour. Between shallow dives, the blue whale surfaces almost horizontally; the blowhole and back appear simultaneously. Its dorsal fin appears fleetingly in comparison with that of a fin whale.

Blue whales are so rare that they are seldom seen except in their Antarctic feeding grounds from December to February.

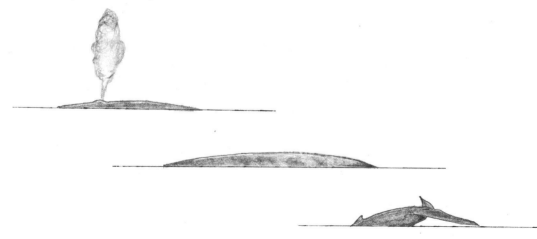

The Minke Whale

(Balaenoptera acutorostrata)

The minke whale (*Balaenoptera acutorostrata*) is the smallest rorqual. It weighs *only* 6 to 8 tons and has an average length of 26 feet. It can be identified by the white patch across the upper side of its flippers and the frequently seen pale gray marks that look like gills above the flippers.

Minke whales are fast swimmers (15–18 mph) and seem to be attracted to ships.

The minke's blow begins under water, and its dorsal fin appears at the same time as its spout.

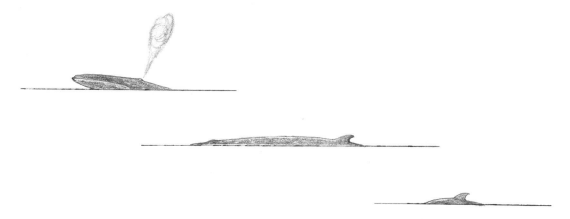

The Sei Whale

(Balaenoptera borealis)

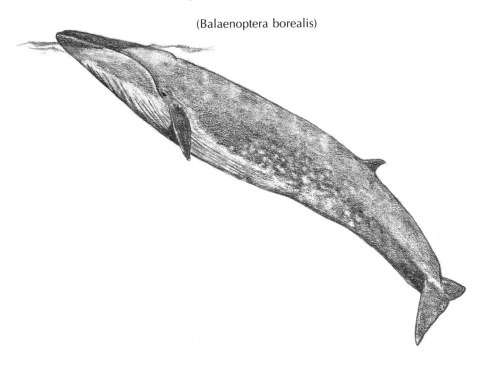

The sei whale (*Balaenoptera borealis*) resembles the minke, but the sei whale is much larger (50 ft., 16 tons). Dark and light spots on its sides and belly, together with its shiny steel gray color, give it a metallic luster in the sea.

The sei whale may be mistaken for a fin whale. Unlike the fin's, however, the sei's entire back appears almost simultaneously as it surfaces and remains visible for a relatively long time.

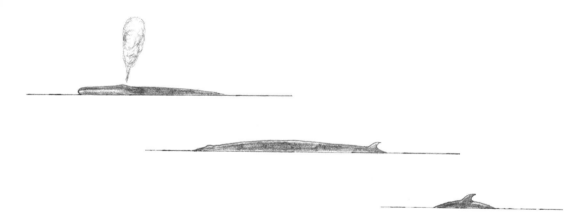

The Humpback Whale

(Megaptera novaeangliae)

The humpback whale (*Megaptera novaeangliae*) has a black back with a white throat and belly. Its scientific name, which means "winged New Englander," arises from the very long, whitish flippers, which are one-third the length of the whale's 50-foot-long body.

This whale's blow is broad and bushy, it is prone to breaching, and it characteristically raises its serrated tail flukes before sounding.

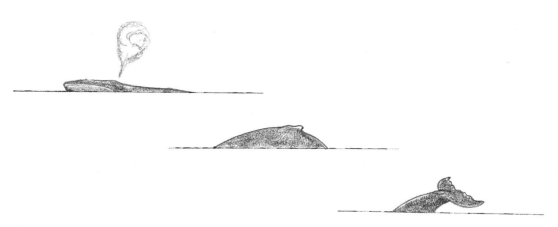

The Toothed Whales: Suborder Odontoceti

The suborder Odontoceti includes sixty-six or more species. These whales have a single blowhole, and all have teeth, at least in some stage of their lives. The species described below are those common to the coastal or near coastal waters off North America.

The Sperm Whale

(Physeter macrocephalus)

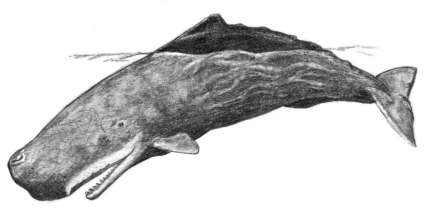

The sperm whale (*Physeter macrocephalus*) is the largest of the toothed whales. The male, which averages 50 feet in length and weighs 40 tons, is much larger than the female (36 ft., 22 tons). The enormous head of the sperm whale distinguishes it from all other species. Its huge, blunt snout projects well beyond its comparatively small lower jaw.

This whale has a blowhole well to the left of midline that produces a spout directed to the left and forward.

Sperm whales prefer the edges of deep ocean trenches where strong currents flow in opposite directions.

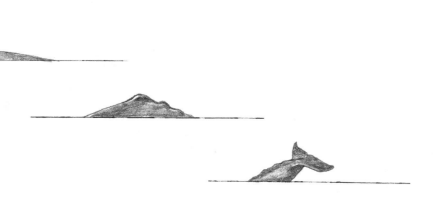

Baird's Beaked Nose or The Giant Bottlenose Whale, also known as The Northern Fourtooth Whale

(Berardius bairdii)

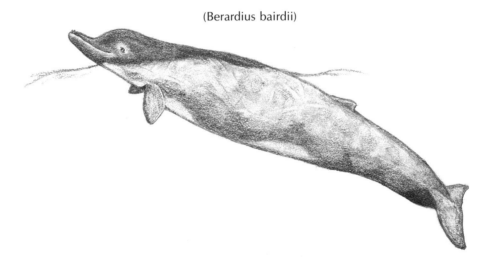

Baird's beaked nose or the giant bottlenose whale, also known as the northern fourtooth whale (*Berardius bairdii*), is the second largest toothed whale. Its average length is 35 feet, and its weight averages 10 tons.

This whale is dark gray with white patches on its belly. The forehead, which rises abruptly from the beak, can be seen when the whale surfaces in alligatorlike fashion with teeth protruding from the extended lower jaw.

Baird's beaked whale tends to be wary of ships but may sometimes be found resting on the surface of the water.

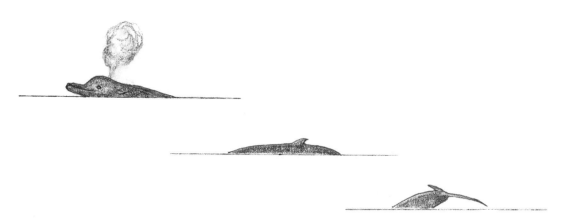

The Goose-beaked Whale or Cuvier's Beaked Whale

(Ziphius cavirostris)

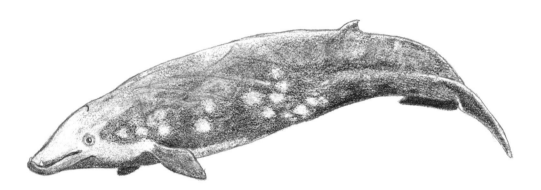

The goose-beaked whale or Cuvier's beaked whale (*Ziphius cavirostris*) is about 22 feet long and weighs 5 tons. These whales travel in groups and raise their foreheads, *not* their beaks, to breathe. They blow immediately in a leisurely way and then as they submerge, they lift their backs, exposing the curved dorsal fin. Before sounding they raise their tails revealing a small notch in the center of their tail flukes.

They are seldom found in water colder than 50°F (10°C).

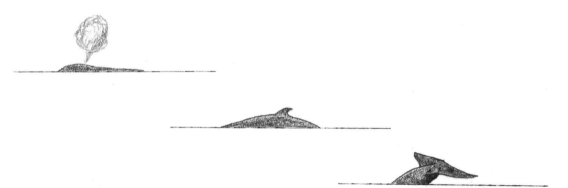

The Northern Bottlenose Whale

(Hyperoodon ampullatus)

The northern bottlenose whale (*Hyperoodon ampullatus*) is readily identified by its conspicuous bulbous forehead, or melon, which resembles that of the bottlenose dolphin, but is much larger.

These whales inhabit deep ocean waters from Rhode Island to the Arctic and respond positively to the sounds of ships.

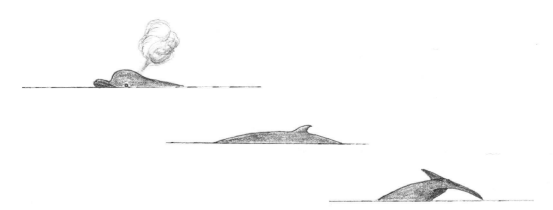

True's Beaked Whale

(Mesoplodon mirus)

True's beaked whale (*Mesoplodon mirus*), blue-gray in color, weighs about 1½ tons. Though these whales inhabit the Gulf Stream, they are seldom seen because they avoid ships and dive quickly when they see or hear bodies not normally found in their environments.

The Male Narwhal, or Unicorn Whale

(Monodon monceros)

The male narwhal, or unicorn whale (*Monodon monoceros*), is easily identified by its conspicuous long (8–10 ft.) tusk. Except for the beluga, it is the only medium-size whale (15 ft., 1.8 tons) in Arctic waters. The narwhals' cylindrical, blotched, olive brown bodies with white bellies lie behind blunt, beakless heads.

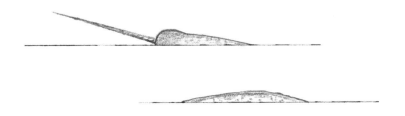

The Beluga Whale, or White Whale

(Delphinapterus leucas)

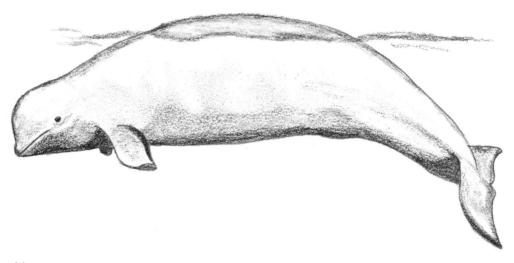

The beluga whale, or white whale *(Delphinapterus leucas),* is nearly pure white as an adult and lives in Arctic waters, although it does migrate as far south as New England and often enters rivers; the St. Lawrence is one of its favorites. In 1966 a beluga, which watchers called Moby Dick, swam up the Rhine as far as central Germany.

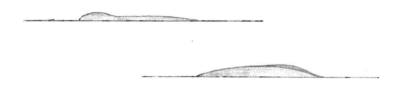

The Harbor Porpoise, or Common Porpoise

(Phocoena phocoena)

The harbor porpoise, or common porpoise (*Phocoena phocoena*), is a small cetacean (5 ft., 190 lb.) with a chunky body and no beak. It is found in shallow coastal waters. A patch of gray or blue skin is found along each flank behind the eyes. The dark flippers lie within the white area of the underside. A dark gray line runs from the front of each flipper to the mouth.

Dall's Porpoise, or True's Porpoise, or The White-Flanked Porpoise

(Phocoenoides dallii)

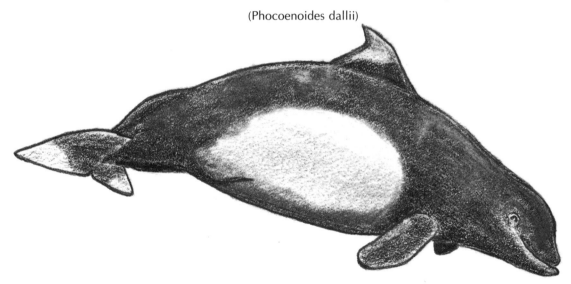

Dall's porpoise, or True's porpoise, or the white-flanked porpoise *(Phocoenoides dallii),* is a small Pacific cetacean about 6 feet long and weighing 270 pounds. Its small, rounded, beakless head has a lower jaw that extends slightly beyond the upper jaw. The dorsal fin with its white edge and backward curve sits a little forward of the center of the animal's black back, which contrasts with its white central surface.

Dall's porpoises are attracted to ships and will ride the bow wave, darting in and out of the wave with jerky, zigzag motions.

The Pilot Whale, or Pothead, or Caa'ing Whale, or Blackfish

(Globicephala melaena)

The pilot whale, or pothead, or caa'ing whale, or blackfish *(globicephala melaena)*, travels in schools of hundreds, often in the company of bottlenose dolphins. These whales swim in geometrical formations, following a leader.

They are black with white or light gray markings on the lower chest and belly. Males are about 20 feet long and weigh more than 4 tons. Females are considerably smaller.

These cetaceans swim in temperate seas, but may migrate to subpolar Atlantic waters in midsummer. They can be identified by their broad-based, curved dorsal fin forward of midback; their long (4 ft.), sharply bent flippers; and their round, broad, dome-shaped foreheads. Their strong tendency to follow a leader may explain the fact that large numbers of pilot whales are often found stranded on beaches.

Globicephala macrorhynchus, the Pacific pilot whale, is similar to the Atlantic species except that its flippers are shorter and are curved rather then bent. It is seldom found out of temperate waters.

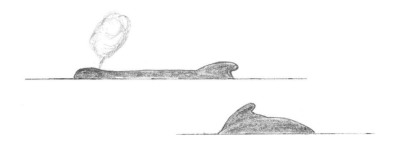

The Orca or Killer Whale

(Orcinus orca)

The orca or killer whale (*Orcinus orca*) is readily identified. Its tall, pointed dorsal fin (up to 6 ft.) shows each time the whale surfaces. The male's fin is upright, even directed slightly forward. The female's fin is curved, more like a shark's.

Male orcas weigh about 6 tons and have an average length of 27 feet. Females are noticeably smaller, but both sexes have a white spot behind the eyes. Their shiny black bodies have white undersides and faint, gray, saddle-shaped markings behind the prominent fin.

These animals will frequently spy-hop to obtain a better view of an approaching boat.

The False Killer Whale, or Lesser Killer Whale

(Pseudorca crassidens)

The false killer whale, or lesser killer whale *(Pseudorca crassidens)*, bears only a superficial resemblance to the killer whale in that its back and fins are similar to those of the female orca. Actually, the killer whale is more often confused with the pilot whale because it is a social animal with a round head, though its head is not nearly so bulbous as that of a pilot whale. Further, unlike pilot whales, false killer whales are attracted to ships and will ride the bow waves of small ships.

When they surface, they show a good part of their 18-foot 2-ton bodies. Often their mouths are open, revealing their large white teeth.

The Pygmy Killer Whale

(Feresa attenuata)

The pygmy killer whale (*Feresa attenuata*) is seldom seen in deep, temperate water. Its slender body tapers significantly behind the tall, curved, dorsal fin like the body of a pilot whale. But its narrow pointed head resembles that of the false killer whale.

It can be distinguished from other whales by its small size (males average 7½ ft., 350 lb.) and its white lips. An expanded white area on the lower lips gives this whale the appearance of having a white goatee.

The Dolphins

Bottlenose dolphin

Dolphins are the most commonly seen cetaceans. They have beaklike snouts and slender, streamlined bodies with triangular fins and notched tails.

The bottlenose dolphin (*Tursiops truncatus*) is the one most widely recognized as TV's famous Flipper. It is small (10 ft., 440 lb.) and wears a permanent "smile."

The rough-toothed dolphin *(Steno bredanensis)* is 8 to 9 feet long and weighs about 300 pounds. It is dark gray with a pinkish hue on the white underside. The long, slender, white-tipped beak with white sides blends into a sloping forehead that gives the animal a sharp, conical, streamlined front end as it moves through warm ocean waters.

These dolphins are a favorite species for trainers because they love puzzles, have long attention spans, and can do complex, prolonged tasks.

The white beak dolphin (Lagenorhynchus albirostris) has a distinct white or pale gray beak and a patchwork of white, gray, and black markings along its flanks. Although they seldom leap out of the water, these animals are powerful swimmers, capable of producing their own bow waves. They are the only dolphins found in the cold waters of the far north Atlantic.

The common dolphin (Delphinus delphis) enjoys bow-riding and leaping alongside ships. Unlike the spinner dolphin (Stenella longirostris), commonly found in aquariums, its leaps do not involve any spinning. A yellow patch on each side and dark lines that run from their flippers to their lower jaws distinguish Delphinus delphis from other dolphins.

Roughtoothed dolphin

White beak dolphin

Common dolphin

63

Whitesided dolphin

The whitesided dolphin *(Lagenorhynchus actus)* has a dark upper surface with a white underside that extends upward to well above the flippers. A gray band extends nearly the length of its body separating the dark upper body from the white below. A yellowish oval patch is found on the sides of this dolphin. It lies below and behind the fin. Part of this patch overlaps the gray band yielding a bright, almost white, region; hence, the name whiteside.

Facts about Whales

"There are substitutes for whale products but not for whales."

Listed below are some interesting facts about whales. If they intrigue you, read on. You may find that there is a lot about whales that you didn't know.

- A blue whale may weigh 200 tons and grow to a length that exceeds 100 feet.
- The tongue of a blue whale weighs as much as an elephant.
- The pleated throat of a blue whale, when expanded to draw water and krill (small shellfish) into its mouth, can increase the whale's total volume by *six times*.
- It takes six months for a human baby to double its weight. A blue whale accomplishes the same feat in one week.
- The largest dinosaur weighed 30 to 35 tons. A blue whale weighs three to six times as much.
- Each tooth in a sperm whale's jaw weighs more than half a pound.
- The intestine of a sperm whale may be 1,200 feet long.
- Baleen whales, the world's largest animals, feed on zooplankton, the world's smallest animals.
- A gray whale migrates more than 10,000 miles each year.
- One humpback whale may carry half a ton of barnacles on its skin.
- A dolphin's 1,700-gram brain is 17 percent larger than a human brain.
- A blue whale's half-ton heart pumps the animal's 7 tons of blood through its 150-ton body.
- A single whale liver contains 5 to 7 pounds of vitamin A.
- In two years a growing blue whale calf converts the zooplankton it eats into more than 15 tons of flesh.
- A blue whale infant calf gains 8½ pounds an hour while drinking 130 gallons of its mother's milk each day.
- A baby whale nurses about forty times each day.
- A nursing mother whale has muscles around her mammary glands that enable her to squirt milk into her infant's mouth.

- A baby whale at birth may weigh one-fifth as much as its mother and be three-fifths as long.
- A 90-ton blue whale eats 4 tons of food each day.
- The long beak of a swordfish is often found in the flesh of a whale.
- The head of a right whale may be one-third its total length.

**A blue whale sipping its supper.
Note its distended throat.**

- Killer whales (orcas) are the only whales that eat warm-blooded animals.
- In 1936 the gray whale population was estimated to be 100 individuals. Today these whales number in excess of 12,000. It is the only whale population to respond so well when protected from slaughter.
- The 2,000 blue whales now found in Antarctic waters represent only 1 percent of the original population.
- The age of a tree can be determined by counting annual rings. The age of some whales can be determined by counting the laminated layers in their waxy ear plug. During the feeding season a layer of keratin-filled cells is deposited in the ear plug. These layers alternate with layers of less dense waxy cells deposited during the part of the year when the whale eats sparingly, if at all. This produces an overall series of laminations that can be counted.
- A Japanese floating whaling factory can cut up and dispatch a 60-ton whale in one hour.
- Connecticut's state animal is the sperm whale.
- So-called killer whales are friendly to humans and are often trained to do tricks at oceanariums.
- A woman thrown into the sea from an exploding yacht feared the worst when she saw three dorsal fins approaching her. Fortunately, the fins belonged to dolphins, which kept her afloat and moved her to a large buoy onto which she climbed and waited for human help.
- Four people were lost in a thick fog off the coast of South Africa in May 1978. They were guided safely through treacherous water by four dolphins, which nudged their boat along. The four men firmly believed the dolphins saved their lives.
- Dolphins and porpoises are cetaceans that look very much alike. There are forty species of dolphins and only six species

of porpoises. Porpoises do not have the pronounced, often "smiling," beaks that characterize dolphins. Dolphins also have cone-shaped teeth; the teeth of porpoises are spade-shaped.

- The echolocation, or "sonar," system of the Ganges River dolphins enables these animals to discern the size, shape, density, position, and velocity of objects so clearly that they navigate and find their food without benefit of sight. All members of the species are blind.

- A blindfolded bottlenose dolphin, using echolocation, can distinguish a 2½-inch from a 2¼-inch ball at a distance of 5 feet.

- The 180-decibel whistle made by a blue whale is the loudest animal sound ever recorded. It equals the noise made by a navy cruiser traveling at normal speed.

- Whales have no vocal cords; yet they can make sounds underwater without releasing any air.

- The low-frequency sounds emitted by some large baleen whales can be heard 1,000 miles away.

- Convergent evolution has led to a similar mouth design for both baleen whales and flamingos. Both have a narrow upper jaw, a large fleshy tongue in a deep lower jaw designed to cover a filtering mechanism that separates food from water.

- Despite the whale's fatty coat of blubber, no fat deposits have ever been found in the arteries of a whale.

- Neither 100-ton whales that live surrounded by water nor tiny kangaroo rats that live in the desert drink water. Both live in environments in which fresh water is not available.

- The blood of whales is less salty than the seawater in which they live.

- Basque whalers discovered North America more than a hundred years before Columbus.

- Ambergris—a waxy substance that develops in large, smelly, laminated lumps around indigestible squid beaks in the intestines of sperm whales—can be used to make perfumes.

- Toothed whales have a single blowhole; baleen whales have two blowholes.

- Whalebone is not bone. It is the baleen found in a whale's mouth and is made of keratin, the same material found in your fingernails.

- Breathing is a conscious activity for whales. If you hold your breath, the carbon dioxide level in your blood increases, and this stimulates you to breathe. If you pass out from lack of oxygen, you start to breathe again automatically. This is not true of whales. Dolphins trapped in tuna nets appear to suffocate. They don't drown.

- A fin whale inhales 3,000 times more air with each breath than you do.

- Air passing out a whale's blowhole may move at a speed of 300 miles per hour.

- Distress calls from an injured whale may attract other whales from 3 or 4 miles away.

- Whales have been observed to herd fish and then take turns eating while their peers keep the fish surrounded.

- After intensive training, Jacques Mayol was able to dive to a depth of 328 feet and hold his breath for 3 minutes and 40 seconds. Sperm whales are believed to be capable of diving to 7,000 feet and not breathing for up to 90 minutes.

Whale Watchers' Questions

"What is a whale?"

The following questions are commonly asked by people on whale-watching cruises. The answers provided are rather brief, but by reading the chapters that follow, you will find more comprehensive answers to these and other questions.

Is a whale a fish or a mammal?

Whalers—and even Herman Melville in his classic *Moby Dick*—refer to whales as giant fish, but, in fact, whales are the world's largest mammals. Like all mammals from the tiny shrew to the giant blue whale, whales have mammary glands. They nurse their young with the milk secreted by these glands; their young are born alive; they are warm-blooded, and they pump that blood with a four-chambered heart as do all mammals. They breathe air that enters and leaves lungs within their chests, but unlike most other mammals, they have very little hair, although hair can be found on the embryos of many whales.

If whales breathe air, why do whales stranded on a beach usually die?

Many people think that stranded whales die immediately because the weight of their own bodies, without the buoyant influence of the sea, crushes their internal organs. This is not true. Whales that have beached often live for several days, and in some cases their lives have been spared (see Chapter 7).

Breathing is difficult for beached whales. Without water to support its body a whale's muscles must work extra hard to expand its chest cavities and thereby draw air into its lungs. A greater problem is the absence of surrounding water that normally carries away the vast amounts of a whale's body heat and also screens the animal from the burning and drying effects of sunlight.

Most beached whales probably succumb to heat prostration, although many that turn on their sides drown when an incoming tide fills their blowholes with water.

Do whales sleep?

Apparently whales do not sleep the way we do. Because breathing is a conscious act for whales, they cannot sleep for very long. They may nap, and often appear to be resting near the surface. Dolphins sometimes appear to sleep, but one eye is always open. Some cetologists think one side of a dolphin's brain sleeps while the other side remains awake to remind the animal to breathe.

What do whales drink?

Strangely, whales, like tiny desert mammals, don't drink anything except some seawater that they may swallow with their food. They can't survive by drinking seawater any more than we can because the salt content of seawater is more concentrated than the fluids in their blood and body cells. If blood or body cells are surrounded by seawater, water will flow out of the cells into the seawater where the salt is more concentrated.

To flush away the extra salt in their seafood diets, whales need lots of water. The water is believed to come from the metabolism or "burning" of fats, which make up a large fraction of a whale's food intake.

How can whales dive to such great depths? When humans do that, they get the bends.

The bends, or caisson disease, occurs in human divers when they ascend too rapidly after working in high-pressure air far below the water's surface. Nitrogen gas, which makes up 78 percent of air, is more soluble in blood and body fluids at high pressure. If the pressure suddenly decreases, the dissolved nitrogen comes out of solution, forming bubbles that can cause severe pain and even death. When a whale dives, the pressure causes its lungs to collapse, forcing the air into the bony nasal cavities of its head. Very little air can enter the blood through these bone-covered cavities. Further, nitrogen is much more soluble in the oily fluid that covers these cavities than in water.

The collapse of the whale's lungs is possible because the animal has no sternum (breastbone). Thus, its free-floating ribs can be squeezed inward, expelling air from the lungs they surround.

How can whales stay underwater for such a long time?

Whale meat is very dark, almost black, because it is rich in myoglobin. Myoglobin is dark red like hemoglobin, the compound found in red blood cells that carry oxygen from our lungs to the cells of our bodies. Myoglobin shares with hemoglobin a capacity for uniting with and storing oxygen. Before a whale dives, it breathes deeply several times, passing inhaled oxygen, via hemoglobin, to the myoglobin in its muscle cells. The oxygen stored in these muscles supplies the extra oxygen needed during the dive.

Do whales talk?

No one knows. They certainly make sounds, and we know that these sounds can attract other whales from well beyond their range of vision. A dolphin will make sounds while other dolphins remain silent. Then a second dolphin will make sounds while the others remain quiet. Are the dolphins talking to one another? Some people think so, but, in fact, the sounds could simply be a signal that indicates, "Hey, I'm here!" It may well be a form of communication, but there is no proof that whales talk the way we do.

How do whales make sounds if they have no vocal cords? And how do they make sounds underwater without releasing air?

Air emerging through the blowhole can make sounds just as you do when you whistle. No one knows for certain how a whale can make sounds without releasing air, but it is believed that muscles around air cavities in the whale's head squeeze on the cavities, setting up vibrations of the enclosed air, which is the source of the sound.

If you hold your nose and keep your mouth closed, you will find that you, too, can make sounds without emitting any air.

Why do whales have bad breath?

People who work closely with whales say that a whale's exhaled air does not have a bad odor. It smells slightly fishy because of the animal's diet and the oily film that emerges with a whale's blow.

Are whales vicious or dangerous to be near?

People who work with whales claim the animals are very gentle. Even killer whales seem to have no interest in devouring humans, though they will gobble up other mammals such as seals and sea lions. Of course, a female whale will protect her calf. Gray female

A whale raises its flukes before sounding near a small ship.

whales have attacked whalers who came between the cows and their calves, and sperm whales have attacked whaling boats or even ships if wounded or harassed. Left alone, whales seem gentle and either passive or friendly depending on the species.

There is danger involved in being near a whale, however. If a whale surfaces beneath a small boat, slaps the water with its tail, or breaches, it can endanger humans, much as we inadvertently endanger ants when we walk near an anthill.

Sperm whales, in particular, seem to have a propensity for resting with only the tip of their snouts above water. It is probably whales in this state that have been most often rammed by ships.

In August 1896 the passenger ship *Seminole* rammed a sperm whale by accident off Sandy Hook, New Jersey. Other sperm whales reacted to the plight of their friend by ramming the ship four times and denting the hull plates and equipment on board so badly that the ship had to return to New York harbor.

In the days of wooden whaling vessels, there were many reports of sperm whales staving in and even sinking ships.

Why do whales spout water?

The air that a whale blows from its lungs is generally much warmer than the air above the sea. The warm exhaled air is very nearly saturated with water vapor, having been in the whale's moist lungs. At cooler temperatures the air cannot hold (dissolve) as much water vapor; consequently, the excess vapor condenses, forming tiny droplets of water that make up the spout. It is analogous to the formation of rain in our atmosphere.

Recent studies on gray whales indicate that a spout does not form with every breath. If you have seen whales in an aquarium, you certainly know that is true of smaller whales. Much of the water that does appear when a gray whale blows is from the water in and around the blowhole that is carried skyward when the whale exhales.

Why do whales become stranded?

There are several possible explanations, but no one knows for certain. Some cetologists believe a parasite damages the navigational sensory organs in the whale's head and the animal, unable to find its way, crashes blindly into a beach. Others claim the whales get caught up in chasing fish and forget to turn on their "sonar," or that their sonar systems are fooled by gently sloping beaches that reflect the sound waves away from rather than toward the whales. Some mass strandings are believed to occur when whales respond to the distress call of one already beached whale, or it could be some mysterious mass suicide to which whales are driven by factors beyond our comprehension. (See Chapter 7 for more theories.)

How can you distinguish between male and female whales?

If a whale is accompanied by a calf, we know it is a female; otherwise, the sex cannot be determined unless you can see the animal's ventral surface. The genital slit of the female whale is close to the anus, and there are also two mammary slits that conceal the whale's nipples on either side of the midline just in front of the anus. The male's genital slit is farther forward so that there is a distinct space between the anus and the genital slit.

At an aquarium where small whales may be seen in glass-walled tanks, you should be able to see these differences and distinguish between male and female whales.

Do whales have belly buttons?

Yes, since whales are mammals, each calf is born with an umbilical cord connecting it to its mother's placenta. After birth, the mother snaps the umbilical cord. It withers away, leaving a belly button.

Again, if you visit an aquarium, you can see the navels on the swimming dolphins and perhaps on other small whales as well.

How long do whales live?

If whales are not slaughtered, they probably live from twenty to seventy years, although it is difficult to determine a living whale's age.

How old must a whale be before it can reproduce?

This depends on the species. Female sperm whales are sexually mature after ten years, but the males do not attain maturity until they are twenty. Dolphins can reproduce after a year or two. For most whales, sexual maturity probably occurs after five or six years.

How many calves do whales have?

Usually whales bear one offspring. Twins do occur, but they are rare.

A Few of the World's Special Giants

"The sperm whale, scientific or poetic, lives not
complete in any literature."

Only in the buoyant waters of the sea could animals as large as whales have evolved. To support the 120 tons of tissue in its body on land a blue whale would require legs with four times the cross-sectional area of those of the largest dinosaur that ever lived. If you have seen dinosaur skeletons in museums, or pictures of these reptiles, you know their legs were already disproportionately heavy.

In this chapter you will have a chance to learn more about a few of the larger whales than would be possible on any single whale-watching cruise.

Blue Whales

Blue whales may reach a length of 100 feet. A record-setting blue whale weighed nearly 200 tons. Such an animal is more than three times the size of the largest dinosaur. It is equivalent in size to a small herd of elephants or to all of the students in a school of two thousand. To truly appreciate its im-mensity, you might walk around the model of a blue whale at the American Museum of Natural History in New York City. These giants of the sea, the largest animals ever to have lived on earth, keep to deep ocean waters. Each summer the remaining few thousand blue whales, from an original stock estimated at nearly 200,000, migrate to polar waters where they feed on a few species of shrimplike krill; each whale devours over four tons of its favorite food each day.

In these cold seas blue whales acquire a thin film of yellow-green diatoms on their skin. This colored film prompted early whalers to name this species the sulfur-bottom.

It is also in polar waters that blue whales have been detected emitting ultrasonic blasts of 20,000 to 30,000 Hz (vibrations per second) as well as their more common low-frequency moans. Perhaps baleen whales have an echolocation system similar to that of their toothed cousins. It may serve them well in finding the highest concentrations of krill.

Blue whale

The sixty to ninety grooves along the blue whale's throat cover more than half its ventral surface. These pleated grooves expand as the blue whale gulps a mouthful of krill. And what a mouthful it is! As the whale's giant pleated bag distends, drawing krill, water, and fish into its mouth, the animal's volume increases six times. A blue whale, mouth full, lying upside down in the ocean as it prepares to spit out the water after straining the krill through its sievelike baleen is an almost unbelievable sight, and one that few have seen.

After the whales have enjoyed four months of gluttonous feeding, the days grow shorter, and the ice pack begins to cover the polar feeding area. The blues then migrate to equatorial waters where they do not eat, or eat very little, because their favorite krill is not found in warm water. The thick coat of blubber they acquired during their four-month feast provides the energy they need until the sun again moves poleward beckoning them to long days of gluttony.

In warm seas they breed, give birth, and nurse and nurture their young. The 130 gallons of milk a calf swallows each day enables it to double its weight in a week as it begins to show the long, sleek, streamlined look of its parents. Such a sleek body enables the blue whale to move through the oceans with a grace and speed that belies its enormous size. But it cannot outswim the faster killer whales who, some report, are fond of the blue whale's flesh. There are tales of killer whales pursuing a pod of blues until finally one old whale, as if a loser in the drawing of lots, falls behind, sacrificing itself to save the other members of the pod.

The swiftness and shyness of blue whales made them inaccessible to early whalers, but their size so attracted modern whalers in fast boats with harpoon cannons that the blue whales' numbers were decimated rather quickly in the twentieth century. In the 1930–31 whaling season alone, thirty thousand blue whales were slaughtered in Antarctic waters. So few remain that many fear the blue whale is on the path to extinction.

The Right Whale

Balaena glacialis in the Bay of Biscay led early Basque fishermen to develop organized whaling. These 50- to 60-foot whales were called right whales because they were the "right" ones to hunt. They were very slow even at their top speed (6 mph), gentle, unafraid, and so rich in oil that they floated even when dead.

Whalers would often harpoon an infant right whale because they knew the calf's mother would respond to her offspring's agony and swim to its aid and into the range of the whalers' iron.

Right whales remain very protective of their young. A cow will swim in a threatening way at a boat that is near her calf but will always veer away before a collision occurs.

On at least one occasion, observers in a small boat were lifted from the water by a right whale's tail flukes. She proceeded to lift and lower the boat and its passengers several times, but in a very gentle way. Was she playing or scolding?

The tender, gentle care offered a right calf by its mother is described by Roger Payne:

I have watched many a calf boisterously playing about its resting mother for hours at a time, sliding off her flukes, wriggling up on her back, covering her blowhole with its tail, breaching against her repeatedly, butting into her flank—all without perceptible response from the mother. When finally she does respond to the torment, it may be only to roll on her back and embrace the infant in her armlike flippers, holding it until it calms down.

Right whales were so easy to capture that by 1750 they were hard to find in the

Right whale

waters off New England where they had once been abundant. Even before that time, in the sixteenth century, when Basque whalers reduced right whales in European waters to the vanishing point, they traveled across the Atlantic to pursue these giants in the coastal waters of northeastern America.

The waters near the Valdés Peninsula in southern Argentina serve as a nursery for a group of right whales from May to December each year. It was here that Roger and Katy Payne saw right whales "sailing." The whales would raise their flukes from the water and set them perpendicular to a strong on-shore wind. Their "sail-tails" would catch the wind and carry them to shallow waters where they would turn around, swim back to deeper water, and set sail again, much as a surfer returns to ride another wave. Whales would spend an entire afternoon sailing. It seemed splendid play for them.

These animals have also been seen lob-tailing and flippering (beating the water with their tails or flippers) or breaching (jumping from the water and then crashing back onto the surface with a mighty splash). When one whale starts this kind of behavior, others often follow suit. Such activity occurs more frequently when the wind fosters lots of wave noise in shallow water—noise with frequencies similar to those in right whales' "voices." Lob-tailing, flippering, and breaching may serve as means of communicating when whales can't "hear" each other's "words." In calmer seas, right whales produce moans of 160 to 230 Hz, belches of 500 Hz, and, sometimes at night, short 2,000-Hz pulses, but there is no evidence that they sing in the manner of the humpbacks.

The Paynes discovered that three distinct right whale populations calve near the Valdés Peninsula. Each group returns once every three years and then disappears into the South Atlantic.

Right whales do not gulp water like blue whales. They do not have the pleated throats common to rorqual whales. Instead, they move at 3 miles per hour with open mouths through shoals of tiny planktonic crustaceans, closing their lips every few minutes and raising their tongues to force out water and capture the zooplankton on the fine hair baleen plates.

In the greatest whaling story every written, *Moby Dick*, Herman Melville describes the great right whale:

Seen from the mast-heads, especially when they paused and were stationary for a while, their vast black forms looked more like lifeless masses of rock than any thing else . . . with him who for the first beholds this species of the leviathans of the sea. And even when recognized at last, their immense magnitude renders it very hard really to believe that such bulky masses of overgrowth can possibly be instinct, in all parts, with the same sort of life that lives in a dog or a horse.

The Humpback Whale

The scientific name of the humpback whale, *Megaptera novaeangliae*, means "big-winged New Englander." It comes from this animal's enormous flippers, which are almost a third of the grown animal's total length of 50 feet. The common name arises from the way it humps its back prior to diving.

Like blue whales, Pacific humpbacks eat their fill in cold (Alaskan) waters during the summer and seem not to feed in their warm calving and breeding waters off Hawaii, where they can be seen by whale watchers from December until April.

While humpbacks are reported not to feed during the winter, the occasional humpback who enjoys tropical waters throughout the year suggests they they may well eat, though more modestly, in warm seas.

Humpbacks are fun to watch and easy to approach. They have no fear of boats and

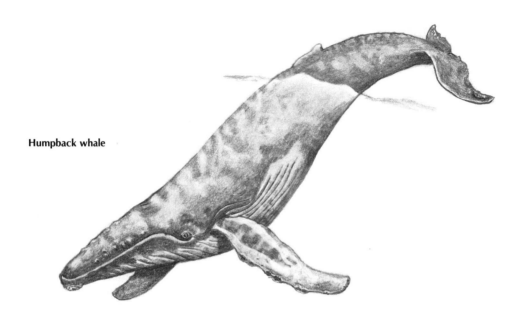

Humpback whale

will often scrape their black backs against the hull of an anchored boat.

They have a propensity for breaching. One was reported to have breached forty times in succession; for what reason, we have no idea. Is it a means of communicating? Is it done to intimidate other whales? Or is it a way of dislodging the manifold lice and barnacles that inhabit the humpback's skin?

Though friendly, frisky, and fun-loving, humpbacks protect their calves zealously. Often a third whale, an "auntie," who is protective joins the cow and calf. Either auntie or mother, who sometimes holds the calf with her flipper, will stay between any boat and the youngster. While protective of their young, they seem not to fear orcas who have been observed following a straight path through a herd of humpbacks.

These whales normally feed by lunging forward, capturing krill, which they strain through their sievelike baleen plates. Several observers, however, have reported seeing one or several humpbacks engaged in another ingenious method of feeding. The humpbacks will dive in unison well below the surface and then swim upward in a wide spiral fashion, releasing a curtain of air bubbles from their blowholes as they ascend. The bubbles encircle a frightened group of small fish and krill, which ascend with the bubbles to the surface. The humpbacks then rise, mouths open, through the appetizing meal.

Observers also report that, while krill are normally difficult to scoop with nets, the process is done with ease when the small animals are within the humpback's bubble mesh.

Steve Morello has a photograph of a bubble mesh released by a fin whale off Cape Cod. From his vantage point aboard *Ranger III*, Steve reports many such sightings. He believes the release of the bubbles attracts fish and squid, making their capture easier. The fin whale does not make a wide encircling mesh like the humpback, but simply a bubble stream.

Steve claims that when he makes a similar, though smaller, bubble pattern during a dive, he finds sand eels and squid gathering around the bubbles.

Killer Whale (Orca)

Killer whales gained their reputation in part from Dr. Daniel Eschricht, who reported finding the remains of fourteen seals and thirteen porpoises in the stomach of one adult orca male. Many interpreted the report to mean the whale ate all these sea mammals at one "sitting," which was not the case. But other observers have confirmed that orcas get their food in a ruthless manner.

One incident reported in *National Geographic* involved thirty killer whales that attacked a 60-foot blue whale. Their actions reflected a clear division of labor. One group stayed under the whale to prevent it from diving, while others tried to cover its blowhole to hinder its breathing. Some chewed away at its dorsal fin, and others devoured its tail flukes. A few nibbled flesh from the tortured animal's lips, perhaps seeking the huge tongue, which is reported to be the orcas' favorite food.

After tormenting this giant and taking turns ripping away flesh from his body, the killer whales suddenly left the blue, still alive, surrounded by its own blood.

Certainly, the sight of a herd of orcas, pointed dorsal fins sticking out of the water to heights as great as 6 feet, as they swim by at speeds up to 30 miles per hour, is awesome and frightening.

There are reports of killer whales who swim in a straight path, seemingly oblivious to anything in their way, surrounding and herding into a circular area a school of salmon. They then take turns eating while the

Killer whale

rest of the herd keeps the fish inside the circular "corral."

These animals, once as dreaded and feared as the lion, have become favorites among some trainers in aquariums because they are so unafraid, intelligent, and trainable. Dolphins are fearful and therefore more difficult to train, but orcas never "worry." They have no natural predators and so seem to have no fear either.

The U.S. Navy has trained killer whales in Deep Ops (Deep Object Recovery) to recover objects from great depths in the ocean and to attach transmitters to these submerged objects.

Since Namu, the friendly killer whale, was captured and seen by the public, fear of orcas has diminished. Trainers now swim beside these animals, ride on their backs, and put their heads inside these whales' open mouths. All this with a "friendly" animal that eats other whales and swallows seals, dolphins, and penguins in one gulp. Killer whales apparently do not regard human beings as part of their diet but seem, rather, to enjoy human company and the music of orchestras. Most trainers, however, carefully avoid an orca when its head moves up and down rapidly. Such movement means watch out, not yes.

When "happy," the orca is readily trained. One female named Ruby learned to say "Rooo Beee." She, in turn, seemed determined to teach her trainer to say "Ku-ooroop." At least that's what he thought Ruby was trying to do.

Even in their natural habitat, these animals are reported to be cooperative. There are tales of orcas helping men hunt humpbacks in return for the tongues of these giants, and of their herding fish to help fishermen.

In Twofold Bay in New South Wales, Australia, according to one report, killer whales would indicate the position of a humpback by leaping out of the water. The whalers would launch a boat and follow the orca, which would stay by the larger whale, leaping on its blowhole to keep it from breathing, or pushing from below to prevent it from sounding.

Once the humpback had been killed, the orca would be allowed to remove the lips and tongue before the carcass was towed to shore.

Whether such tales are true or whether the tellers of such stories correctly interpreted the events they observed are open to question, but there can be no question that humans are fortunate in not being a part of orcas' warm-blooded diet.

Gray Whales

More people have seen gray whales than any other species. Each year thousands of gray whales migrate along the shallow waters off Washington, Oregon, and California, where they can be seen by whale watchers standing on coastal cliffs. Those who want a closer view can board whale-watching boats or even journey by air, land, and sea to lagoons along the shores of the Baja Peninsula.

After their 6,000-mile trip from the Bering Sea where they feed voraciously all summer, building up a thick layer of blubber, these 50-foot long, 35-ton, cigar-shaped giants seek a warm, shallow lagoon in which to give birth to the young they have carried within their wombs for a year. The nearly blubberless whale calves would have little chance for survival in the cold waters off Alaska. Hence the survival of this species requires that they move southward for calving. Why they choose the shallow Baja lagoons is not known, but it is a protected warm-water area to which they seem attracted each year. It is here that they mate as well as give birth, and it may well be that their return to these lagoons each year ensures that boy meets girl. In fact, their annual trek southward to Baja may explain why this species has recovered so dramatically after being virtually extinct twice within the last century. The failure of the great right whale to regain its numbers despite protection may stem from the fact that these whales have no "love lagoons" to ensure that males and females

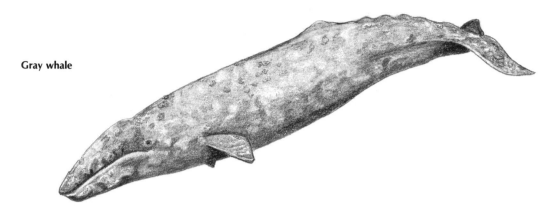

Gray whale

meet. In vaster waters, a male right whale may not meet a female at the proper time.

At least one whale authority, however, feels that grays never were as diminished in number as some think. He maintains that their migration paths and mating and calving grounds change periodically.

A mother gray is very protective of her newborn calf and will caress its body with her flippers and carry the 15-foot-long, 1½-ton infant on her back. Often she will blow bubbles beneath the calf in a blow-and-bounce-the-baby behavior, or she may slide under her calf, rolling and bouncing the infant in the ocean waters.

Early whalers referred to gray whales as devil fish or hard heads because they would fiercely defend their young, often ramming their heads into a whaling boat.

It was in the lagoons of Baja California that Captain Charles Melville Scammond discovered the grays in such abundance in 1857. Though he tried to keep secret how he managed to return to port so quickly with a ship full of oil and whalebone, his crew soon spread the word. By 1880 the gray population in Baja had dwindled to a few hundred.

Whale watchers who enter Scammond's Lagoon today are often able to reach out and touch these gray giants who, when viewed closely, are seen to be black but so covered with white blotchy scars and barnacles that from a distance they appear gray. They can be approached from the rear in a motorboat, provided the motor speed doesn't change, but woe to the observer who comes between a cow and her calf.

The females that breed here return the following year to give birth in the lagoon where the calf was conceived. The pregnant cow traveling north in springtime is much thinner than when she arrived, but once she reaches the cold Alaskan waters where her male friends are already feeding, she begins to rebuild the insulating layers of blubber she needs for energy. She will roll on her side and scoop power-shovel helpings of shrimp, crabs, clams and other organisms from the bottom of shallow ocean areas. Then, rearing upright, she forces water through her ba-leen plates with pistonlike thrusts of her 1½-ton tongue while her upright position allows gravity to help force food into her stomach. While some maintain that grays eat only in colder waters, other observers claim to have seen grays feeding in Baja's waters, and still others claim that gray whales will not pass up any food they encounter along their migration route.

Like all whales, grays lack vocal cords, and many believed them to be mute, but oceangoing gray whales have been heard emitting pulsed signals with a frequency of 12,000 Hz—sounds that may provide them a means of echolocation.

Gray whales are now known only in Pacific waters, but Pleistocene remains of gray whales in estuaries of Sweden, southern England, and the Netherlands indicate that gray whales lived in the shallow waters of the Atlantic during the high seas of the interglacial periods. During these periods there may have been more extensive connections between oceans.

Some believe grays lived in the Atlantic until historic times. Others claim they are still in these waters though their numbers are very small. Such beliefs are based on a 1725 report in *Philosophical Transactions* in which Paul Dudley wrote:

The Scragg whale is near kin to the Finback, but instead of a fin . . . his back is scragged with half a dozen knobs or Nuckles; he is nearest the Right Whale in Figure and for Quantity of Oil, his Bone (baleen) is white but won't split.

The scragg whales, some claimed, were Atlantic gray whales, but most cetologists argue that scraggs were simply small right or humpback whales.

So, whale watchers, keep your eyes open! A gray whale seen in Atlantic waters would surprise most authorities.

Sperm Whales

Many humans spend a third of their lives growing up and acquiring the education they need to pursue a profession. The time from birth to puberty constitutes nearly one-fifth of the human life span. The long childhood of *Homo sapiens* is a characteristic we share

Sperm whale

with *Physeter macrocephalus* (sometimes known as *Physeter catodon),* whose body shape serves as a symbol of the Hartford Whalers hockey team.

A sperm whale's gestation period is sixteen months. By that time the full-term fetus is 12 to 14 feet long and weighs a ton.

During birth the cow often "stands" upright in the water, her blowhole above the surface. A group of sperm whale midwives, heads inward, surround her, offering protection and help. In a similar way, sperm whales often attend an injured member of a pod. When a calf is attacked by killer whales, sperm whales surround the youngster with their heads outward, perhaps to pick out by echolocation the approaching enemy.

A baby sperm whale's huge tongue allows it to swallow the bursts of milk that the mother squirts into its long, toothless mouth.

After two years of nursing, calves begin to catch their own squid and fish. Soon after they learn to feed themselves, the young males begin to group together apart from the harem, which consists of twenty to thirty females, many of whom are pregnant or lactating. By age ten the females, which are considerably smaller than males, are fertile, but the young males, which may still occasionally take a gulp of milk, do not generally appear sexually mature until they are twenty. At this age these young bulls, which are about 40 feet long and weigh 30 tons, undergo a growth spurt that adds another 10 to 20 or more tons of flesh. The young males, ten to forty years old, form bachelor pods of as many as fifty bulls. They are apparently excluded from the harem when they reach sexual maturity. During the summer, perhaps because their larger size demands a heartier diet, they leave temperate waters, where the harems remain, to seek food in polar seas.

As winter and the breeding season approach, bachelor pods move toward the equator. One large, older male generally attains breeding rights to a female pod or harem. He will defend his right against all male intruders from bachelor pods. His defense often involves fierce fights during which the bulls ram their enormous heads together, slap each other with their tails, or hold and rip at each other's jaws. Often the relatively small lower jaws are broken in these battles. The deformed lower jaw attributed to Moby Dick, the world's most famous sperm whale, was probably the result of such a battle.

The slow maturation of sperm whales is further evident in their teething. These Odontocetes have no teeth for their first four to five years. The set of fifteen to thirty pairs of lower teeth is not complete until they are thirty to forty years old. Their upper teeth, which may begin to appear at age twenty, are often never fully complete.

Without teeth, or with relatively few teeth, and with underwater speeds of less than 15 miles per hour, how do young sperm whales catch the giant, fast, maneuverable squid on whom they prey deep beneath the surface of the sea? Because sperm whales often surface very close to where they began their dive,

many cetologists think the whale simply waits quietly near the ocean floor until a luminescent squid moves close to its giant head. At that point the whale closes its jaws and sucks in the trapped prey.

Other cetologists believe that sperm whales create powerful sonic pulses that can stun squid from a distance. Dolphins seem to have a similar mechanism. Observers find that as dolphins pursue a school of fish, the fish, which at first are frisky and darting about, begin to slow down, moving aimlessly about as if drugged. It may be that the dolphin's sonar beams have stunned them. One theory holds that sound generated within the sperm whale's giant spermaceti-filled snout can be reflected back and forth much as a laser builds up a powerful pulse by multiple reflections of coherent light. When the sac at the front of the animal's snout is made transparent to sound by periodically eliminating air from one small region, the amplified high-frequency pulse may be powerful enough to stun a squid, making its capture easier. The fact that the time between a sperm whale's clicks is related to the length of its head and so enables a listener to predict the whale's size offers support for such a theory.

Many have wondered why squid, living at depths where no light can penetrate, release a dark ink, since blocking light is of no value in an already dark environment. Proponents of the theory that sperm whales have a sonic "laser beam" suggest that the ink may reflect the sperm whale's sound waves, and thus serves as a defense mechanism by reflecting sound, not light.

High-frequency bursts of sound, or clicks, at twenty to eighty per second are the most common sounds from sperm whales, but they also emit roars, moans, and groans when beached and perhaps in the sea as well. A squeal from a baby sperm whale that was struck accidentally by Jacques Cousteau's research ship *Calypso* attracted adult sperm whales over a radius of 7 miles.

But how can these whales who were prized by whalers because they floated when dead, descend to depths of 7,000 feet? How do they overcome their buoyancy?

The weight of a sperm whale's head, which makes up one-third of its weight and as much as 40 percent of its length, is only 12 percent skull bone. The bulk of its head is the spermaceti organ, a muscle and oil-filled connective tissue. Many cetologists believe it is spermaceti that allows a sperm whale to change its density and, therefore, descend and ascend through water with ease.

In air, spermaceti oil, which is a liquid at 91°F (33°C), changes to a soft, crystalline solid below 88°F (31°C). At the same time, the density of the material increases and continues to increase as the temperature of the solid drops. One theory maintains that because cold water can enter nasal passages, it can cool the spermaceti oil, increasing its density and thus reducing the whale's buoyancy. This effect can be enhanced by constricting blood vessels that carry warm blood to the spermaceti organ.

When the whale is ready to ascend after a long dive, dilation of blood vessels to the spermaceti organ could melt the solidified oil, causing a decrease in density that buoys the animal upward. Detailed calculations seem to confirm the idea that heat losses through the skin and to the cold water in the nasal passages when related to temperature, pressure, and changes in water density at various depths could control a sperm whale's density and enable the animal to descend at 5 miles per hour and rise at slightly greater speeds.

With 20-pound brains, an elaborate social structure, a highly developed "laser" echolocation system, and an apparent means of communicating over long distances, these animals may be the most intelligent in the oceans. Some believe they may possess a culture, though this theory seems to be based more on admiration for a unique animal than on firm evidence.

Beluga Whales

Known as sea canaries to early sailors, these mammals emit squeals of varied frequencies that can be heard above the sea's surface. They also produce a bell tone unique among whales, whistles of 3,000 to 9,000 Hz, and echolocating clicks. In addition, they make what appear to be threatening sounds by snapping their jaws together.

Beluga whale

These white whales are actually gray at birth. By age six their color has changed gradually through ivory tones to a white that has a purity broken only by traces of pigment on the edges of flippers and flukes.

Belugas are generally docile and can be viewed at close range in a number of aquariums.

They enjoy a diet of smelt, herring, salmon, squid, shrimp, and annelid worms. Their fondness for cod causes them to swim as far south as New England from Arctic waters.

Belugas have three things to fear: orcas, polar bears, and entrapment within the Arctic ice pack. The Invit Eskimos wait for white whales trapped under ice to surface at openings where they easily kill them as they rise to breathe.

Polar bears, too, are often seen waiting for beluga near an opening in the ice pack. As the whale's blowhole emerges from the icy water, the bear delivers a blow to the white whale's head that knocks him senseless.

There are reports of belugas using their finless but crested backs or their oil-filled melons (foreheads) to break through ice four inches thick.

At aquariums, where these animals are trained, they seem to love to have their gums rubbed, and trainers delight in having the whales demonstrate the frequency range of their voices. By alternately covering the whale's blowhole with a hand as the animal "talks," the trainer can show that the sound comes from the blowhole and not the mouth. Of course, belugas can also make sounds without emitting any air.

Dolphins

In 1938, when Marineland of Florida opened its gates near St. Augustine, the owners used beautifully colored fish to attract customers. People came by the thousands, but not to see the fish. They were attracted by the dolphins who stole the show. These animals would

toss shells to customers and play catch with them.

Recognizing the attractiveness of the ever present smiling dolphin, Marineland hired Adolf Froher to train these animals. Their tricks became Marineland's main attraction.

After World War II, other marinelands and aquariums procured dolphins as crowd pleasers. By watching these animals and reinforcing desired behavior with a fish reward, trainers were able to develop a wide repertoire of dolphin tricks.

Trainers were impressed to find that dolphins could learn tricks by watching another dolphin who had previously mastered the feat.

Dolphins can learn a great variety of tricks, in part, because they love to play, learn, and be in the company of humans. They will play catch, toss and catch a Frisbee, toss rings, shoot baskets by leaping from the water to dunk a shot, and even carry people on their backs.

Marineland shows and Flipper's TV fame led millions to visit other marinelands and aquariums to marvel at the feats of these amazing mammals.

One trainer found that dolphins could be taught to remove trash from the aquarium. For each piece of trash delivered, a dolphin received a fish as a reward. When cleaning time arrived, the dolphins would exchange collected trash for food. One bottlenose dolphin named Mr. Spock seemed to find far more trash than his peers did. After a few sessions, the trainer put a "tail" on Mr. Spock. He discovered that this dolphin, during his free time, had collected and hidden a huge pile of debris in a remote corner of the aquarium. When cleaning time arrived, Mr. Spock would bring one piece of trash from his savings account, get a reward, and then return to his bank for another piece of trash that he could cash in for fish.

When an eel, chased by hungry dolphins, escaped by swimming into a hole at the bottom of the pool, one of the dolphins captured a fish with a poison sting and put it into the hole. The eel immediately emerged back into the pool, and the dolphins resumed the chase.

Such ingenuity may indicate that dolphins have the capacity for thoughtful planning, but scientists who study dolphins differ in their assessments of this animal's intelligence. Some think they are no more intelligent than dogs; others equate them with primates; a few believe they may have a language that allows them to communicate in a manner similar to, or superior to, our own. A very few think their language enables them to transmit a form of culture so that, like humans, each generation of cetaceans does not have to rediscover all that is known.

Their brains have many convolutions, and the cerebral cortexes of these organs have one and a half times as many cells as ours.

In their natural environment they are gregarious and have a social hierarchy, a pecking order, that establishes who is subservient to (and swims below) whom. Some researchers who have studied dolphins are convinced that a herd will sometimes banish an unruly dolphin. Such isolation may cause the animal to die of loneliness. Although this belief is unverified, captive dolphins do seem depressed when isolated and clearly excited when reunited with their peers.

Identifying whistles seem to aid them in locating one another and maintaining proper spacing as they herd fish in the ocean. In coastal areas, they wisely stay in shallow water to avoid the attacks of orcas.

Because dolphins and tuna are often found in the same waters, fishermen are apt to net dolphins along with tuna. Regulations require that the nets be made of a fine mesh so dolphins won't get entangled. The nets also must have a "super apron" that allows surfacing dolphins to escape.

A peculiar whistle from a female dolphin giving birth brings a dolphin midwife to the scene. As soon as the 3½-foot-long, 30-pound infant leaves the birth canal, the midwife helps the mother move the baby to the surface where it inhales its first breath. For the next several weeks, the auntie dolphin stays near the mother, helping her guard and play with the baby.

Several swimmers claim they were saved by dolphins. Caught in a rip current and struggling for shore, one man went under only to be lifted back to the surface and pushed to shore by a dolphin.

Even in natural settings, dolphins seem to like people. One of the most famous love affairs between humans and dolphins is the story of Opo, a female bottlenose dolphin, who appeared in Hokianga Harbor, New Zealand, in 1955. She followed boats around the harbor and later frequented the beach near the little town of Opononi. There she would swim and frolic with bathers, especially children with whom she played ball and to whom she gave "horsie rides." If a child became too rough, she would swim away and protest by slapping her tail on the water, never against a human body. Her joyful ways led children to call her "our gay dolphin."

Opo's fame spread through New Zealand. Tourists flocked to Opononi to see and photograph the playful, gentle dolphin. A sign near the beach read, "Welcome to Opononi, but don't try to shoot our Gay Dolphin."

One day in the spring of 1956, Opo did not appear at the beach. A search found her wedged between rocks where she had died. No one knew for certain what had happened, though some people believed she had been stunned by an explosion of gelignite that fishermen used to kill fish.

Opo was pulled to shore where she was buried in a marked grave covered with flowers.

Whale Biology

"Ten or fifteen gallons of blood are thrown out of the heart at a stroke, with immense velocity."

The anatomy, physiology, and behavior of whales never ceases to amaze us. There is so much about whales that we don't know, and they are so difficult to study in their natural habitats that cetology is really in its infancy. We don't even know how long these animals live. Roger Payne's method of identifying whales by their individual markings will help establish reliable data on life span, migration routes, breeding habits, and so forth. But these are long-range studies that will require time and the cooperation of many scientists and whale watchers.

Anatomy

Cetaceans differ from one another dramatically in shape, size, color, and markings, but all have lungs and a blowhole at the top of the body through which air enters and leaves. All have a four-chambered heart, warm blood, and a smooth, thin, sensitive skin that is often scarred and always subject to sunburn if out of water for more than a few minutes. Wounds of the skin that heal rapidly in the whale's natural environment can lead to blood poisoning in captivity. In fresh water, the skin swells and softens, producing a pulpy, ulcerated mass of flesh.

The skin of rorqual whales is often marked with shallow pits as if a sharp spoon had been used to scoop out the flesh. The pits are made by a small tropical shark that uses its suckers to latch on to the whale's skin and then sink its lower teeth beneath the skin. Water flowing over the whale causes the shark to rotate. As it turns, its sharp teeth, buried in the whale's skin, carve out plugs of flesh.

The skin of many whales, particularly the slow-moving baleen whales, is covered with barnacles and parasites. In polar waters, the blue whale's skin is often covered with greenish yellow algae.

Beneath the skin is a layer of blubber, a fatty tissue that serves to insulate the body and provide a storehouse of food for migrating whales.

Whales are streamlined, but, unlike fish, their bodies are round and torpedo-shaped. In many whales, the neck vertebrae are fused, giving the animal the appearance of having no separation between head and body. Whales' tail flukes are always horizontal, and their forelimbs have been modified into flippers. Some whales still have vestigial hind limbs and, in a few cases, these "legs" are even visible externally.

Life in water does not require strong bones, so a whale's skeleton represents only 17 percent of its body weight. Animals as large as baleen whales could not exist on land. To see why, consider what happens when the dimensions of a body double. Doubling the height, length, and width increases surface area four times, while volume (and, therefore, weight) increases by a factor of eight.

Consider a whale 10 times the length, width, and thickness of a human. Its surface area would be 100 times yours; its weight, 1,000 times greater than yours (about 70 tons). With 1,000 times more flesh produc-ing heat, and with only 100 times as much surface area to conduct that heat away, such a whale can lose heat only one-tenth as fast as we do per pound of flesh. To survive, it must live in water, which can carry away the animal's heat far better than air can.

Or consider the legs needed to support such an animal on land. Since bone strength is proportional to cross-sectional area, the legs of this giant would have to be, not 10 times as wide as ours, but 32 times as wide. (The square of 32 is about 1,000.) What a strange-looking beast it would be!

You see now why the largest land animals (dinosaurs) had oversized legs and lived in swamps where much of their weight was supported by the buoyancy supplied by water.

Baleen whales have thin, fibrous plates that hang from their upper jaw inside the mouth. Shaped like scalene triangles with smooth outer edges and frayed, fibrous-lined inner edges, these plates serve to trap the small zooplankton and fish that the whales take into their mouths. The baleen is an ex-

Baleen plates like this hang from the palates of the toothless baleen whales. Some bowhead whales have baleen plates that are 14 feet long.

tension of the ridges found in the roof-of-the-mouth lining in many mammals. In bowheads and right whales, the large lower lip encloses dark baleen plates. These plates, while only ¼-inch thick, may be as long as 14 feet in bowheads. The number of baleen plates in a whale's mouth varies from 150 in gray whales to 400 in bowheads. The baleen fibers intermesh with neighboring plates to form a sievelike strainer.

The muscles in front of a whale's tail drive the animal forward by providing the energy for the power stroke as the animal moves its flukes upward. The downstroke is passive, serving only to put the flukes in position for the powerful upstroke.

Folds in a dolphin's skin enable it to maintain laminar (nonturbulent) flow over its body at speeds of 20 knots (23 mph). Many think that a dolphin's leaping from the water is an indication of its playful nature, but if the dolphin surfaced only part of its body to expose its blowholes, the turbulence would reduce its speed and take more of its energy. Leaping, for a dolphin, is an adaptation for easy movement. It is a matter of efficiency of motion, not sport.

Ingestion and Digestion

Herman Melville described the feeding of baleen whales when he wrote, "Numbers of Right Whales . . . with open jaws sluggishly swam through the brit [crustaceans] which, adhering to the fringing fibres of that wondrous Venetian blind in their mouths, was in that manner separated from the water that escaped at the lip. As morning mowers . . . these monsters swam, making a strange, grassy cutting sound; and leaving behind them endless swaths of blue upon the yellow sea."

The bowheads and right whales are skimmers. They swim through krill with their mouths open, capturing crustaceans and small fish in their baleen sieves as water flows between the fibers. Periodically they will close their mouths and use their tongues to scrape food off the fibrous baleen and toss it down their throats.

Unlike the skimming rights and bowheads, the rorquals are gulpers. Their baleen plates are shorter, but their pleated throats, with forty to a hundred grooves, act like a bellows that sucks in huge amounts of water with fish and krill. The *cavum ventrale* (ventral cave) of the blue whale—the cavity that separates the pleated furrows of the throat from the internal body wall—can expand the front half of the animal's body from 3,800 to 34,000 cubic feet. After such a giant gulp, the whale rises to the surface upside down and squirts the water through its baleen.

Humpbacks often herd fish and krill by encircling them with bubble nets as described in Chapter 5. Gray whales also herd fish by circling maneuvers, after which they swim vertically upward, open-mouthed, through the center of the school, catapulting from the sea with fish falling from the sides of their mouths.

Gray whales have smaller heads and shorter baleen plates than right and bowhead whales, and they have only a couple of grooves beneath their throats. Their lack of special adaptations leads biologists to regard gray whales as more primitive than other whales, but their mechanisms for ingesting food may be related to the greater variety of food in their diets. They will eat fish, krill, shellfish, worms, and even vegetation, according to some observers.

The gray whale usually rolls on its side to feed, and each animal seems to have a favored side onto which it turns when gouging shellfish from the bottom of a shallow area.

Steve Morello, a naturalist aboard the *Ranger III* out of Provincetown, Massachusetts, believes that humpback whales also bottom feed. His photographs clearly show scrape marks on humpbacks, and he reports that they often rise with mud along their jaws. This suggests that these whales may slide their mouths along the ocean bottom.

Blue whales generally eat four times a day. At each meal they consume a ton of their favorite krill (*Euphausia superla*), which lives in cold polar seas. In warmer waters, they do not eat the lobster krill that other baleen whales relish and that is tasty to human palates as well. Fin whales consume three tons of krill per day, humpbacks about two tons and seis about one and one-third tons. Over the course of a year at the turn of the century, when whales were still abundant, these four species alone ate 150 million tons of Antarctic krill.

Many biologists attribute the increase in krill-eating blue whiting fish and seals to the increased krill available since the dramatic decline in the whale population began three decades ago.

The toothed whales flourish on a diet mainly of fish. For killer whales, who will often play cruelly with a captured sea lion much as a cat toys with a mouse, the diet also includes seals, birds, porpoises, and even large whales.

Many odontocetes have very few teeth; they crush their prey with strong jaws before

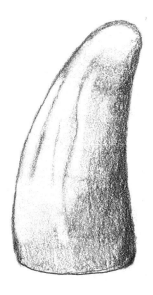

A sperm whale tooth.

swallowing. Even sperm whales have no teeth until they are mature and yet are able to capture and swallow giant squid.

The swallowed food enters a four-chambered stomach. The first chamber is really a sac-shaped, dilatable extension of the esophagus, much like a bird's crop. It contains no digestive glands. When it is opened by whalers, as much as a ton of krill may spill onto the deck. The second chamber is thick-walled with a folded lining rich in digestive glands that secrete into the cavity. It is here that food is mixed with digestive juices. The third chamber seems to be merely a connection to the fourth chamber, which is lined with digestive glands.

Digestion continues in the intestine, which is five to six times as long as the whale's body and fifteen to sixteen times the body length in sperm whales.

The liver has no underlying gall bladder, but a pancreas secretes digestive juices into the intestine.

Digested food is absorbed from the intestine by blood-filled capillaries in the folded intestinal lining. Undigested waste is excreted as flakelike feces through the anus.

Respiration and Circulation

When we breathe, we inhale only about 500 milliliters (a pint) of air. This is but one-fourth the total volume of air in our lungs, which make up 7 percent of our body weight. (A whale's lungs are less than 3 percent of its body weight.) A fin whale exchanges 3,000 times as much air with each breath. This constitutes 80 to 90 percent of the air in its lungs.

As in all mammals, blood flowing through the lungs absorbs oxygen from the air. But, unlike other mammals, cetaceans are not forced to breathe when the carbon dioxide level in their blood rises. If you hold your breath until you pass out, your breathing will automatically start again. If you are under water, this action will draw water into your lungs. This is not the case with whales. Dolphins trapped in tuna nets will actually suffocate from lack of oxygen. They do not drown by breathing water.

Blood from the lungs and elsewhere is pumped throughout the whale's body by a huge four-chambered heart that seems unique in having a shunt between two major coronary arteries, a vessel that, if present in humans, would reduce the danger of heart attacks and the need for bypass surgery. Yet, dissections of cetaceans reveal none of the fatty deposits found in human arteries.

To cope with long dives, cetaceans have a large blood-to-body-weight ratio, blood gas sensors that respond only to very high carbon dioxide concentrations, and a great tolerance for the lactic acid that builds up in muscles that do not receive sufficient oxygen. Also, their muscles are rich in myoglobin, which enables them to store large amounts of oxygen within muscle tissue.

Further, during dives, blood is diverted from external areas to the heart and brain. This reduces the metabolic rate, and therefore oxygen needs diminish. The pulse of a whale in a dive may fall from twenty-four to eight beats per minute.

In addition to a lack of sweat glands, an ability to shut off blood flow to its skin, and an insulating layer of blubber, whales also conserve heat by virtue of their small surface-area-to-weight ratio. These heat-conserving mechanisms enable whales to thrive in cold polar waters where humans would die of hypothermia in several minutes.

Whales also possess a counter-current system of blood vessels so that arteries carrying warm blood from the heart to exterior muscles and skin are intertwined with veins carrying cool blood from the periphery of the body. This heat exchange cools the warm blood before it reaches regions near the body's surface where it will lose heat to the cooler surrounding water. Since heat losses are proportional to the temperature difference between warm and cool bodies, the reduction in a whale's peripheral blood temperature decreases the heat flowing from blood to water.

Excretion

Though surrounded by water, whales can no more meet their water needs by drinking seawater than can shipwrecked sailors on a life raft. Their body cells have a lower salt concentration than seawater does, which means that water will flow from their tissues into the sea. How then do whales survive? What do they drink to replace their water losses?

Most cetologists believe that whales obtain their water by metabolizing fat. This process releases larger amounts of water than does the oxidation of proteins and carbohydrates. The high fat, low sugar content of whale milk and the fatty diet and stored blubber of adult whales make water unnecessary. They get all the water they need when they burn fat.

Experiments in which seawater was placed in a dolphin's stomach showed that the animal's feces had a salt concentration equal to its blood. This meant that water must have moved from body cells into the intestine until the salt concentration of the seawater there was the same as that in the animal's blood.

To flush away the extra salt in their salty seafood diets, whales need lots of water. We think the water comes from fat. There is no evidence that whales have special cells to excrete salt the way fish do. Some seabirds have salt-excreting cells near their beaks. Whales may have such special cells, too, but if they exist, we haven't found them.

To keep their blood and body cells at a salt concentration similar to that of other mammals, whales are believed to excrete large amounts of urine containing salt dissolved in water. The kidneys of large whales have as many as 3,000 lobules. These lobules are believed to contain the glomeruli, or extraction units, needed to remove the salt that builds up in their blood as they eat salty krill and fish and, in the process, swallow some salt water. This is borne out by the high kidney-to-body-weight ratio and by the fact that freshwater dolphins have only about one-third as many lobules in their kidneys as do dolphins that live in the sea.

Reproduction

Like all mammals, whales reproduce sexually and bear their young alive. The mating process in animals as large as whales is not easy, and many attempts are often required before a cow is impregnated. In gray whales, mating involves three animals. A second male, not involved in the actual sexual union, holds the other male and the female in place, so they do not slip away from one another in the buoyant water. In view of the gray whale's resurgent population, this method seems to be successful.

Since whales are believed to have little if any ability to smell, cetologists wonder how a male whale can tell that a female is in heat. Among many mammals, the odor of the secretions produced by a female in heat serves to attract male suitors. It may be that these secretions can be tasted in the water flowing over a whale's baleen. Others believe the female makes her state known by sounds or behavior patterns.

In most male mammals the testes that produce the sperm cells are in a scrotal sac outside the body. This ensures that the testes are several degrees cooler than body temperature, a requirement essential to the production of active sperm cells in most mammals.

Whales, however, carry their testes inside the body in keeping with their general streamlined shape. Apparently, body temperature does not inhibit the formation of sperm cells in cetaceans.

The penis of a male whale is also normally withdrawn within the walls of the genital slit through which it can be extended for urination and mating.

As might be expected with animals as intelligent as whales, courtship among cetaceans is extensive. They stroke each other with their flippers, nuzzle, nibble, and swim side by side, showing the affection associated with courtship.

Union of sperm and egg produces a ½-millimeter ($\frac{1}{50}$ inch) wide zygote that begins to divide and becomes implanted in the cow's uterus. Generally, within a year this tiny cell has grown to a fetus that may weigh more than a ton.

When the embryo is about an inch long, the hind limbs that begin to form, reflecting the land animal ancestry of the species, are resorbed. When the embryo is about a foot in length, its forelimbs develop into flippers, and tail flukes appear. During the last three months of the gestation period, the fetus simply grows and grows and grows.

Normally, large mammals carry a fetus for a long time. The gestation period for a horse is eleven months; for a rhinoceros, eighteen months; and for an elephant, twenty-two months. Yet, cetaceans, the largest of all animals, produce enormous calves after relatively short gestation periods. This may reflect their high metabolic rate. Cows return from their summer feeding grounds fat and healthy, with plenty of energy available for calving or lactating.

Gestation periods among whales vary from eight months for porpoises to sixteen months for sperm whales. Most are from ten to twelve months. Even a blue whale cow carries her calf for only eleven months.

The young odontocetes are usually born tail first. This was believed to be an adaptation to prevent the infant from drowning, since water might enter its blowhole during a head-first delivery. However, observers report a number of successful mysticete births in which the infants were delivered head first. Apparently, tail-first delivery is not essential for survival and may be the normal mode among baleen whales.

After delivery, the mother whale will move sharply to break the umbilical cord. Then, often with the aid of an attending whale, she will push the calf to the surface for its first breath.

Cows remain very close to their calves during the nursing period. Few things are more beautiful to an avid whale watcher than to see cow and calf emerge from the sea simultaneously, produce a double blow, and then submerge together.

Young calves nurse for brief periods about forty times a day. The cow is equipped with muscles that enable her to push her nipples

Mother and baby bowhead moving slowly through Arctic waters.

through mammary slits on either side of her body just in front of the anus. The calf, which lacks both the capacity to submerge for very long and a mouth that can suck milk, surrounds the exposed nipple with its mouth. The cow then contracts muscles that squirt a huge stream of milk into the calf's throat. The calf swallows and returns to the surface for air.

The fat, rich milk is said to taste like a mixture of fish, liver, milk of magnesia, and castor oil. One might guess the taster was not enthusiastic about future sales of whale's milk in the marketplace, but baby whales seem to enjoy and thrive on it. They gain as much as 200 pounds per day, and drink up to 130 gallons of the fatty fluid in the same time span.

Calves nurse for periods of six months to two years, depending on the species.

Because of their long gestation and lactation periods, sperm whales are believed to calve only once every three years. Humpback cows produce about two calves in three years, while gray whales may calve annually—a factor in their rapid recovery from virtual extinction.

Compared with land mammals, cetaceans are slow in breeding and attaining maturity, despite a rapid growth rate both as fetuses and as infants. Their life spans, when not interrupted by whalers, are believed to be quite long, although the age of a whale is difficult to determine.

Senses and Nervous System

Like all mammals, the whale has a large brain and spinal cord that carries messages to and from all parts of the body. Nerves from their sensory organs provide these animals with information about their environment.

Humans rely principally on sight to gain

information about the world outside the body; dogs rely heavily on smell in their sensory world; bats, like whales, use their keen sense of hearing to assess their surroundings.

Vision is of limited value to whales. Water is often murky, and very little light penetrates below 30 feet where whales are often found in search of a meal.

When light passes from air to the fluid interior of a land mammal's eye, it is bent (refracted) sharply at the eye's surface, the cornea. You can see this effect by looking at a pencil partially submerged in a glass of water. The pencil will appear to be sharply bent owing to the refraction of light passing from water to air.

The lens in your eye serves to bend light even more and focus it into images on the sensitive retina at the rear of the eyeball. But a whale must form images from light passing from water, not air, into its eye. Such light is refracted very little by the animal's cornea. To compensate for this difference, the eye of a whale is similar to that of a fish in having a lens that is nearly spherical. Such a lens can bend light sharply as do the highly curved lenses in a microscope.

Life in the sea negates the need for tear glands, but whales do secrete an oily substance much as we secrete tears. The oil protects the eye from the friction created when water streams over it as the whale moves through the sea. The eyeball itself is very thick and tough to prevent it from collapsing from the pressure at great depths. Further, a tapetum, a reflecting layer of cells, lies behind the retina to bring as much of the dim light as possible onto the retina. A similar layer in the eyes of cats explains why their eyes shine in the dark.

Whales, then, can use their eyes reasonably well in shallow water, and dolphins, which are capable of reducing the size of their pupils to tiny slits in air, can see as well out of water as they can beneath its surface. Only dolphins among the cetaceans have eyes set far enough forward so they can see objects in front of them with both eyes, a capacity essential for the stereoscopic vision that allows for depth perception. The brain, by synthesizing the two images, one from each eye, which are slightly different, produces an image that appears three dimensional.

To understand the importance of stereoscopic vision, try covering one of your own eyes as you move about. Be careful; you will find your ability to judge distance has been greatly reduced.

Whalers were able to approach resting whales from either directly in front or directly behind because whales, with eyes on the sides of their giant heads, cannot see anything ahead of or behind them.

When approaching from these positions, whalers had to be very quiet, for whales have a very keen sense of hearing. In fact, whales use this sense to obtain information and probably to form mental images of the environment and the organisms around them.

The internal ear of a whale is similar to that of any mammal; however, whales have no external ears. The meatus, a tube leading from a mammal's body surface to its middle ear, is present in whales, though narrow, and filled with a laminated ear plug where it widens before reaching the middle ear. An elongated finger-shaped eardrum separates the middle ear from the meatus.

Sound vibrations traveling in water pass down the meatus to the eardrum. As this membrane vibrates in response to the sound, the bony ossicles of the middle ear, which are connected to the eardrum, respond, amplifying and transferring the sound to the cochlea of the inner ear. Here nerve cells are stimulated and carry impulses to the brain.

To prevent the buildup of high pressure within the middle ear, mammals have a tube (the eustachian tube) that connects the middle ear with the throat.

Despite the fact that the tube seems to promote ear infections by providing a pathway for bacteria from the throat, it does allow air to move from the middle ear to the outside, thus keeping the pressure within the middle ear the same as that of the atmosphere. Sometimes, in an airplane or in a car on a trip through the mountains, you will swallow to open the eustachian tube and relieve the pressure difference that you can feel in your ear.

A whale's eustachian tube ends in the air sacs in its head; it does *not* connect with the animal's throat. During a dive, pressure on the air sacs forces air through the tube into the middle ear to compensate for rising pressure from the deep water outside the body. An additional compensatory mechanism is provided by two muscles attached through ligaments to the eardrum. By increasing the tension of the eardrum, the pressure inside and outside the middle ear can be made equal.

To prevent the transfer of sound from the skull bones to the middle ear, an effect that makes hearing underwater difficult for humans, the whale's ear is insulated from the hard bones of the skull by connective tissue, which is a poor conductor of sound. Further, the space between the middle ear and the skull is filled with an oily foam that offers yet another barrier to sound transmission.

These adaptations for receiving sound, coupled with the whale cochlea's particular sensitivity to high-pitched vibrations, enables these mammals to hear and respond to many sounds, including the high-frequency reflected clicks of their echolocation system.

Smell is probably of minimal value to whales. Toothed whales have no organs of smell, no olfactory nerve, and no olfactory lobes in their brains. Baleen whales have a small organ of smell, an olfactory nerve, and a small olfactory bulb in their brains, so they can probably detect smells when they blow.

The sense of taste may be present in

whales, but little is known about it. Generally, animals that swallow food whole, as whales do, have little sense of taste.

The presence of pits and hair follicles around the mouths of some whales, their fondness for being petted and stroked, and the close contact between cow and calf all suggest that whales have a well-developed sense of touch.

7

Whale Psychology

"Mind in the waters"

The playful behavior of whales "sailing," tails uplifted in the surf as the wind carries them shoreward, would suggest that whales are a cut above your average mammal. This belief is reinforced by the attention and TLC that a mother whale lavishes on her calf, and by the response of whales to the cries of distress from another that is injured or disabled. Whales appear to be loving, caring, sensitive animals—more human than some humans.

How much of a whale's behavior is learned and how much is instinctive? Such a question is difficult to answer, but the size and structure of this animal's brain indicates a high degree of intelligence.

But why do we consider some animals, such as chimpanzees, more intelligent than others? Primarily because chimps seem capable of handling abstractions, of solving problems that require new behavior or insight.

A chimpanzee in a cage will use a stick to pull in a banana that is beyond its reach outside the cage. Somehow, the chimp can see the solution to its hunger. It says (to itself), "Aha! If I use that stick, I can reach the banana!" Other animals show less capacity for handling such problems.

Dolphins, as you know from Chapter 5, do exhibit such behavior, and this fact, coupled with their big brains, makes us think they are intelligent. Yet, if these animals are so smart, why do they wind up stranded on beaches?

How Smart Are Whales?

Human intelligence is so closely related to our spoken and written language and to our prehensile (grasping) hands that we find it difficult to conceive of an intelligence that has no written language, buildings, or artifacts that can convey culture from one generation to the next. Yet cetaceans, which have no need to build in their nomadic lifestyle, and which lack hands with opposable thumbs that make both building and writing possible, do seem to be capable of communicating, though at what level we don't know.

The brains of most whales are far larger than ours, but, of course, they are much bigger than we are, and brain size in mammals is related to surface area, with some exceptions. Dolphins, which are comparable though somewhat larger in size than humans, have brains that are slightly larger than ours.

Many biologists and psychologists believe that the number of layers, laminations, folds, and convolutions of the brain's cerebral cortex is related to an animal's intelligence. Though the laminations in a dolphin's brain are not well developed, there are four layers of cells just as in humans, and the cortex is as convoluted and folded as ours. Dolphin brains differ from human brains in the regions of the organ that show extensive development.

In humans the cerebral areas that control muscle action and speech are highly developed, as would be expected. The dolphin's brain is developed in those areas that seem related to sensitivity to sound, impulses from the facial areas, and social involvement (interaction with others).

Cetaceans may be as intelligent as humans. Some think they are more intelligent but in a different way, a way that we can't imagine. Our intelligence depends on muscular activity—building, writing, reading, and speaking. These activities, which enable us to transmit culture, mark a breakthrough in the course of evolution.

It took two million years for humans to evolve physically. In less than ten thousand years we have moved culturally from the Stone Age to the Atomic Age. Our capacity for transmitting knowledge through symbols negates the need for each generation to rediscover all that is known, or to do all that must be done to make human culture possible.

It is our combined ability to generate a culture through time, which vastly exceeds the capacity of any single brain to produce or fully comprehend it, that identifies *Homo sapiens* today.

Cetaceans may be able to communicate the acoustic images they "see" to other whales by retransmitting the received echoes that give rise to these images. Such a capacity may require an abundance of brain cells that have nothing to do with intelligence.

The fact that dolphins have been known to help humans in distress led to the idea that they have a special affinity for us and, perhaps, share in our powers of reason and language. However, a dolphin saving a drowning human may merely reflect that animal's instinctive habit of boosting the sick or newborn members of its own species to the surface where they can breathe.

Echolocation, which seems to be the whale's way of gaining an awareness of its surroundings, is an ability it shares with the bat, an animal not widely regarded as exceptionally intelligent.

The other sounds that whales emit may well serve as signals that summon or warn others and serve as a means of identifying themselves or their state of being. Chimpanzees will drum on a tree trunk with a stick to indicate to others, "Hey I've found a lot of good food over here. Come join me."

Even dogs and cats, through barks, growls, purrs, and body positions can signal anger, fear, happiness, and other emotions. No one doubts that cetaceans possess a system of communication comparable to those of other life forms. But can they communicate by symbols? Can they transmit "ideas"? Do the sounds and hand signals that trainers use to convey short sentences to dolphins indicate that these animals possess a capacity for dealing with symbols and language, or are the dolphins' actions the result of conditioned responses done in expectation of a reward?

If intelligence is the ability to use a learned pattern of activity in a new context, then dolphins are certainly intelligent. Any form of activity normal to a dolphin seems capable of being transferred through training to situations totally outside the normal behavior pattern of dolphins. For instance, a dolphin will leap 18 feet above the water to touch a suspended ball; yet, dolphins don't normally obtain food or anything else in this manner. They have "learned" to use their leaping skill to obtain a reward (food).

By reinforcing a particular activity common to dolphin behavior with an immediate reward or with a whistle, which dolphins have learned to associate with a reward, we can teach dolphins and other whales and sea mammals to do all kinds of amazing tricks. They will retrieve a ball, play catch, shoot baskets, leap through hoops alone or in groups, leap, spin, breach, make sounds on command, and even stand up and "walk" by making their powerful tails move back and forth forcefully and rapidly, thus lifting and moving the rest of their bodies horizontally across the water.

Such behavior, while entertaining, seems to many a reflection of these animals' agility and capacity for conditioning rather than an indication of intelligence. The dolphin Mr. Spock, who learned *by himself* to store trash in order to obtain a reward, is a better example of real intelligence. Another example of intelligent behavior involves a false killer whale and a dolphin that lived in adjoining tanks at an aquarium. Since they apparently preferred to swim together, the whale, when no humans were about, would move the barrier between the tanks so the dolphin could leap over it and join him. The whale seemed to know his behavior was "illegal," because he would do it only when no one was around.

Should we train whales? Many cetologists think we should not. Even though training attracts people to see whales, the animals trained must be caught and transported to aquariums. In the process, some whales die. Those that survive often develop symptoms of stress—ulcers, low food intake, depression, low resistance, and so forth. Pneumonia and other diseases are common among captured cetaceans, which must be

Two trained bottlenose dolphins leap into the air and together traverse a suspended bar high above the spectators below.

protected from eating the "garbage" thrown to them by well-meaning but ignorant observers who do not realize that cetaceans have finicky digestive systems.

The intelligence of whales remains a mystery. Their many "friendly," humanlike behavior patterns tend to make us think they "should be" intelligent. After all, any animal that smiles all the time must know something that we don't. But just how intelligent they really are is subject to debate. Some equate a whale's intelligence with that of a dog or cat; others compare it with that of a chimpanzee; a few maintain that those large brains house an intellect greater than, but very different from, our own.

Stranding

If whales are intelligent, why do they do something as foolish as swimming onto a beach? Again, no one knows for certain, but we are beginning to develop some theories.

In 1976 an injured false killer whale was found aground in the Dry Tortugas Coral Bank. Thirty more whales were milling about their stranded friend. James Porter swam in among the whales. He found that whenever he made a noise that sounded like a whale with a waterlogged blowhole, a whale would immediately swim under him and lift him to the surface.

After the grounded whale died, the other whales were able to swim away at high tide because of the steeply sloped beach. On another beach, the entire herd might have been stranded.

An injured whale may seek a place where it can breathe without having to use any of its dwindling energy supply for swimming. Finding a beach that meets this need, it strands itself and continues to release its distress signal. Other whales responding to the signal become stranded beside the injured animal. In many cases, the whale may recover and slip back into deeper water with a high tide or through the aid of other whales. We find only the whales that do not make it back.

Such a theory may seem reasonable, but not all strandings involve an injured whale. Various other theories have been developed to explain the beaching of whales:

A right whale stranded on a beach.

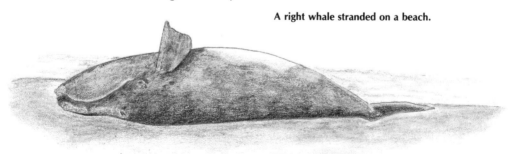

1. The echoes from a cetacean's echolocation system are reflected forward along gently sloping beaches. The whales think they are in very deep water because they hear no echo and so continue swimming shoreward.
2. The animals, in panic, are fleeing sharks or orcas.
3. The whales, for reasons we can't comprehend, are deliberately attempting mass suicide.
4. Their pursuit of small fish leads them into shallow waters.
5. Polluted water interferes with their sensing system, and they are unaware of the fact that they are in shallow water.
6. A species of roundworm that infests whales damages their navigational sensory organs, and they become disoriented.

New Zealand cetologist, Frank Robson, has offered some new insights into strandings on the basis of careful observations. First, he separates strandings into mass and single strandings. A single stranding may involve one whale, a cow, and calf, or a cow, calf, and attending female.

A type one stranding in Robson's system involves a single whale that has cuts and bruises about its head. Autopsies on such whales show that parasites have invaded the animal's inner ear or nasal cavity near the blowhole. Robson hypothesizes that in an attempt to relieve the intense earache or dislodge the pain-producing parasite, the whale bashed its head repeatedly on rocks or a reef. Then, exhausted and bleeding, it drifted into shallow water.

Type two strandings involve old or sick whales that fall behind the rest of a herd during migration. If their route is along coastal waters, they may be carried to a beach by the shoreward velocity of breaking waves. If the sick or old whale is accompanied by a calf and attending female, they too may be stranded.

In both types it seems likely that unless the whales are isolated, distress calls from the stranded whales might bring others to the scene, leading to larger strandings.

Type three strandings occur after healthy whales are observed swimming in close circles. Suddenly, one whale will break away, move toward shore, and become stranded. This whale, upon becoming stranded, issues a distress signal. Soon there is a mass stranding as other whales respond to the signal.

Type three strandings seem to involve social problems within the herd. The milling of the herd in circles before the "expulsion" of one member seems to be a type of trial or rite associated with the individual that is finally banished. When such an event occurs on the high seas, the evicted whale may wander off and die or join a new herd. In coastal waters, the potential for stranding exists if the whale swims shoreward in a state of confusion, depression, and anxiety.

Type four strandings occur only with migrating bachelor herds of sperm whales. The stranded males all seem to be 42 to 48 feet long and are driven shoreward by fierce winds and treacherous currents.

The remaining bachelors show no inclination to help their brethren in distress. This seems to be a part of the rugged individualism practiced by these bachelor herds into which adolescent male sperm whales are driven by the tranquil harem herds.

The differences in the "morality" of sperm whales were known to early whalers and were clearly expressed by Melville in *Moby Dick*: "Say you strike a Forty-barrel-bull-poor devil! All his comrades quit him. But strike a member of the harem school, and her companions swim around her with every token of concern, sometimes lingering so near her and so long, as themselves to fall prey."

Attempts to save beached whales frequently fail. If dragged into deeper water, they will often return and strand again, leading some to believe the whales have a "death wish." But on occasion, such strandings are successfully terminated.

One such case occurred on April 15, 1981, when a young 25-foot sperm whale stranded at Coney Island, New York. He was pushed away from shore by the tide and later found in the surf off Oak Beach. The New York Stranding Network and the U.S. Coast Guard towed the whale to a boat basin where he lay or swam slowly, attracting visitors who soon named him Physty—because of his feisty nature and his species name, *Physeter macrocephalus.*

As Physty rested on his right side with left eye and pectoral fin above the surface, he emitted grunts, groans, squeaks, coughs, and a variety of clicks. The clicks seemed to emerge in beamlike fashion from a small oval area at the top of his huge snout.

During the first week, Physty received three injections of penicillin after swab tests from his blowhole revealed bacterial infections and parasites. As he lay in the water, he used his sonarlike beam to "see" some of the 50,000 people who came to see him. By the eighth day, he was very weak and lay grounded at low tide. Hundreds watched in silence as his breathing weakened, fearing that each breath might be his last. But as darkness fell, he began to rally. By the next morning he was swallowing medicated squid and swimming about the basin.

As several thousand shouted, "Go, Physty, go!" the young whale was escorted to sea. Physty had survived!

Should you find a beached whale, look to see if it has been damaged physically. If it appears to be in satisfactory condition, and if you can turn the animal, right the whale so its weight is evenly distributed. Then call for assistance as discussed in Chapter 2.

While waiting for help, keep the whale's skin moist to reduce chances of sunburn and heat prostration. If enough cloth is available, cover the whale's back with damp sheets, clothing, or whatever, but be sure to *keep water away from its blowhole*. Some people foolishly think the whale has to have water in its blowhole so it can spout. Also keep people off the whale's body. It has all it can do to lift its ribs without having to raise people too.

Beached whales may sometimes be helped and may survive, as the story of Physty illustrates. Even if they die, they provide cetologists with an opportunity to learn more about these animals.

Whales on the Move

"To the gull's way and the whale's way where the wind's like a whetted knife."

Whaling ships often sighted herds of sperm whales moving along a compass course at speeds beyond the capability of the pursuing vessels. These animals appeared to be migrating, but from where to where?

The first systematic attempt to map the seasonal migration of whales was that of C. H. Townsend. He pored over the ungrammatical misspelled records in the logbooks of American whaling voyages from 1761 to 1920. He mapped the time and place of capture of 36,908 sperm whales. The data revealed that members of this species are spread across the oceans, but they seemed to congregate in those areas that were the "fishing" grounds of whalers. Townsend's findings were incomplete. Whalers did not cruise randomly across the sea. They sailed to those regions where whales had been found before. However, more recent scientific analyses of sperm whale movements and locations confirm Townsend's study. Whalers really did know where and when to find whales.

During this century, cetologists have marked more than five thousand whales. They do this by firing a marked stainless steel pin, nearly a foot long, into the whale's blubber. The location and time of each marking is recorded. Only a few hundred of the pins have been recovered by whalers as they flensed (stripped the blubber from) the captured animals. But those that were found indicate that whales follow a north–south migration pattern and tend to return to the same area year after year.

A more humane and accurate system has been developed by Roger Payne and others who point out that individual whales have very distinct color patterns on their flukes, flippers, heads, and bodies. By keeping a record of such sightings through photographs and drawings, it should be possible to find where individual whales move from season to season. Such a method has already established that, while whales tend to return to the same winter habitats each year, humpbacks from Hawaii do intermingle with humpbacks from the eastern Pacific during the summer.

Sperm whales gather where warm tropical

waters collide with cold polar currents. In those locations, particularly off the west coast of South America and the southwest coast of Africa, squid, the sperm whale's favorite food, is abundant.

Male sperm whales migrate farther into polar waters than do the smaller females and their calves. Herds of bulls are often found in cold waters, far from any females.

We know more about gray whale migrations than we do about the movements of any other species because grays follow the California coast to the Baja peninsula where they mate and give birth before returning to the Bering Sea during the warmer months. Some whales travel as far as 15,000 miles in one round trip. Because gray whales seem to follow a shallow-water path along America's West Coast, some scientists think these whales may navigate by following ocean-bottom contours, offshore islands, and promontories. The procession is always led by older whales, suggesting that a learning process may be involved. Once in the warmer waters off Southern California, the southbound whales begin to probe inlets, searching for their shallow-water breeding grounds. Perhaps the warmer water sets off a complex reflex reaction that initiates their search for "home."

Humpback whales can be found from May to November feeding in Glacier Bay, off Alaska, or in the western waters of the North Atlantic. The Atlantic humpbacks spend their winters 2,000 miles to the South on the ocean banks north of the Dominican Republic. During April and May, as they migrate northward, they sing their characteristic songs in the beautiful emerald waters off Bermuda. In the late spring and summer, they can be found along the New England coast. Studies done by the Cetacean Research Program at the Center for Coastal Studies in Provincetown, Massachusetts, indicate that a very large percentage of the same humpbacks return to these New England waters each spring.

Pacific humpbacks follow southward paths in the winter. One path takes them to Hawaiian waters, another to the area off

A herd of migrating sperm whales could outrun sailing ships.

Southern California, and others to the Cape Verde Islands, and the Lesser Antilles.

Many believe that humpbacks are such gluttons in the summertime that they do not eat during the winter but concentrate instead on singing and breeding, activities they do not perform extensively in the summer. It used to be thought that humpbacks sing only in warm water, but there was a recent report of humpbacks singing in Glacier Bay.

There are several herds of right whales, though their numbers are small. The population of right whales in the eastern Atlantic was nearly wiped out by the sixteenth century. Basque whalers then sought these animals off the coast of Newfoundland where a small herd of about two hundred still spends its summers feeding in the Gulf of Maine, the Bay of Fundy, and off the coast of Nova Scotia. It is believed that these are the same whales found off the coast of Florida in the winter.

It was the right whales' tendency to migrate along coastal waters that led to their demise, for they were very accessible to whalers out of eastern ports.

Some southern right whales are known to winter in the protected Golfo San José in Argentina, and are believed to move toward Antarctica in the summer. There are as many as 350 right whales off the Cape of Good Hope, and about 150 along the New Zealand coast.

Some conservationists are optimistic about the survival of right whales. If their numbers do increase, we may be able to learn more about their migratory routes.

When Antarctic seas are bathed in sunlight twenty-four hours a day during December and January, the remaining southern blue whales gorge themselves on krill. As the sun moves northward and autumn arrives in the Southern Hemisphere, the blue whales migrate, following the sun toward the equator. Their thick layers of blubber, acquired during the summer feast, are sufficient to meet their nutritional needs during the long winter fast.

Bowheads, narwhales, and belugas spend the entire year in cold Arctic waters. They are the few species of whales that do not seem to migrate, although many toothed whales are believed to be guided in their migration simply by their food supply.

But what serves as a compass for the gray whales along their 10,000- to 15,000-mile round trip? And what directs humpback, right, and blue whales along less well known migratory routes? Do they follow a leader as many whales seem to do? If so, how does the leader chart the course? What triggers whales to begin their migrations?

Many believe shorter days tell the whales it is time to move toward the equator. Shorter days may set off a nervous response that initiates the move, or perhaps diminishing food supplies or cooling seas provide the stimulus that leads whales to think, "What are we doing here? With enough blubber to last a year, why should we stay in this cold water when we could be enjoying the warmer waters of the Caribbean or Hawaii?"

But once they decide to migrate, what map do they follow? Do they, like birds, have a built-in magnetic compass that enables them to orient themselves relative to the earth's magnetic field? Or do they navigate like bees, using the sun to set their course?

Gray and right whales may follow natural landmarks and ocean contours in the shallow coastal waters through which they move. They may have learned their routes by following older whales in previous migrations.

Whales that follow a more dispersed, meandering pattern of migration may follow calls from one another. Their sounds can be heard for hundreds of miles, and it may be that certain sounds to whales mean, "Hey, follow this sound and you'll find warmer water" or "Come this way; there's enough krill for an army of whales."

At this point in time, little is known about how whales migrate. We know something about when and where they go, but whalers knew that centuries ago. Why they follow the paths they do and what serves them as a compass are questions that remain unanswered.

Whale Sounds, Songs, and Talk

"If you were to make little fishes talk, they would talk like whales."

Many people would like to have Superman's X-ray vision. Whales certainly don't have X-ray vision. In fact, whales can't see very well, but they do have X-ray hearing. They emit high-frequency sounds that are reflected just like the waves emitted by sonar and radar transmitters. Whales can hear the sounds reflected by various objects and can thereby locate these bodies even in murky water. Experiments with dolphins indicate that their sonar enables them to distinguish between 2½- and 2¼-inch balls at a distance of 5 feet.

Whale Songs

In the nineteenth century, the port of Lahaina in Maui was a station for whaling vessels. Today boatloads of whale watchers leave the port in search of humpback whales that come to these Hawaiian waters each winter to give birth, court, and mate.

Beneath the beautiful waters off this emerald in the sea, a diver spots a solitary humpback at rest. Its long flippers hang down, its body rests, tilted at 45 degrees. As the diver quietly approaches the whale, he can "feel" this giant's song. The air in his body cavities—his lungs, his mouth, his sinuses—resonates with the booming sounds from the singing whale. Yet, no bubbles rise from the animal's blowhole or mouth.

Roger Payne and Scott McVay first recorded the humpback's songs near Bermuda, where humpbacks gather on their way north each spring. You can hear recordings of these songs on some whale-watching ships, or you can buy the same Capitol records that they are probably playing: SW 620, *Songs of the Humpback Whale*, or ST-11598, *Deep Voices*. A small record with humpback songs was also included in the January 1978 issue of *National Geographic* in connection with an article entitled "The Gentle Whales."

How do whales, which lack vocal cords, make sounds? The lack of bubbles from sing-

A male humpback sings his "bubbleless" song.

ing whales shows that they emit no air. Close both your nose and mouth. You will be surprised to find that you, too, can make sounds without letting air escape from your lungs. Air vibrating within the cavities of their heads enables whales to make sounds that can be heard hundreds of miles away.

The song of the humpback is a series of about six themes that follow one another in a fixed order. Scientists who study the humpbacks' songs find that all male members of the herd sing the same song, independently, a song that, when played fourteen times faster than it is sung, sounds like a bird's song.

The fact that only males sing and that songs are seldom heard except during the breeding season as solos, never as a chorus, suggests the song may be a love song. Yet, if the singing is related to courtship, why do the whales sing only when alone? Are they longing for love?

Although all members of a herd sing the same song, the songs of different herds, while somewhat similar, are also clearly different.

Those who have listened to humpbacks singing through the winter from year to year hear the same song in the late fall that was heard in early spring when the whales left their winter retreats and headed north to feed. In other words, they return singing the same songs they sang six months before, songs that last as long as thirty minutes, songs the whale has stored in its memory for half a year. But as winter passes, the humpback's song slowly changes. New phrases are sung at greater speed than older ones. A new phrase often combines the end and beginning of an old phrase in which the middle has dropped out, much as we might contract the words "do not" to "don't." Humpbacks appear to be composers as well as singers.

Scientists studying the humpback's evolving song have discovered fourteen simple, predictive laws governing the modification of the songs. These laws hold for all humpback herds. Apparently humpbacks inherit or learn rules that enable them to compose as they sing. Their ability to memorize the "words" of a thirty-minute song and store that information for six months led Roger Payne to say, "To me, this suggests an impressive mental ability and a possible route in the future to assess the intelligence of whales."

Other Sounds in the Sea

Not all whales sing, but they all make sounds. Because water is a better conductor of sound than air, whale sounds travel over great distances at four times the speed of sound in air and with little loss in energy. Thus whales are bathed in a vast variety of noises transmitted by the sea. The eerie melodies that lured mythical mariners to shipwreck were probably the sounds of whales. When one is enclosed in a wooden hull that will conduct sounds from the sea, it is impossible to locate the source of the sound. It seems to come from everywhere.

During World War II, submarine sonar operators listened for enemy ships, expecting to hear few other noises. The operators were confused by a great variety of beeps, groans, croaks, crackles, whistles, and moans.

Biologists called to the project discovered that not only whales but even fish make sounds. Toadfish and triggerfish set up vibrations within their air bladders. Squirrel fish, parrot fish, and porcupine fish create sounds by grinding their teeth.

Soon sonar operators learned to distinguish among the many sounds they heard. In addition to the songs of the humpbacks, they heard very low rumbling sounds of 20 Hz coming from fin whales, and 100- to 200-Hz thumps emitted by piked whales. Baleen whales produced 20- to 200-Hz moans that lasted as long as 30 seconds. Also heard were short, low-frequency thumps from right, bowhead, gray, fin, and piked whales;

higher-frequency (1,000 Hz and greater) chirps and whistles of 0.1 second or less duration; and clicks with frequencies as great as 30,000 Hz that last for less than 0.01 second are believed to originate in gray, fin, sei, blue, and humpback whales. Such sounds are so distinctive that individual whales can be recognized.

The loud sounds from baleen whales are reflected by large bodies beneath the sea. The echoes returned to the whales may aid them in finding their way through murky water. There is no evidence that mysticetes have evolved sonar systems as efficient as those of odontocetes, but they must have some such system to find their food and make their way through the sea.

Sonar-Equipped Whales

The 20-Hz sounds of baleen whales have wavelengths greater than 200 feet. Such sound waves will travel great distances. Such large waves curl (diffract) around even large objects and continue along their paths. But some odontocetes seem capable of detecting objects as small as 0.015 inch by listening for the echoes of the high-frequency (200,000 Hz) sounds they emit. These sound like a series of clicks to us and are emitted in clusters of up to 1,000 per second. Some dolphins seem capable of emitting two very different frequencies simultaneously.

Early Greek philosophers thought that we saw things by sending out light signals from our eyes. The light was reflected by objects back to our eyes, enabling us to see them. We know now that light reflected to our eyes originates not in our eyes but in luminous objects such as the sun. But the Greeks' explanation of vision is a good account of the workings of the odontocetes' echolocation system.

The sonar systems of various toothed whales have been studied most closely in small whales restricted to the tanks of an aquarium. These whales use four main types of echolocation. Porpoises emit a narrow band of relatively low-frequency sound waves with a peak energy at less than 4,000 Hz. Orcas also emit low-frequency sounds of a broader range that peaks at 16,000 to 20,000 Hz. The widely studied bottlenose dolphin emits high-frequency waves with a peak energy between 30,000 and 60,000 Hz. River dolphins emit the highest frequency sounds with a peak ultrasonic energy near 100,000 Hz.

Dolphins sweep their sound beams over the target by turning their heads as they emit sounds; then they listen for the echoes. So sensitive is their echolocation that they can differentiate between copper and aluminum, plastic and glass, and can detect small differences in the size of objects. Apparently the vibration of air in their nasal passages is the source of these sounds.

The domed, bulbous melon of the toothed whale is believed to be a means of focusing sound waves into a beam, just as a concave mirror in a searchlight produces a beam of light.

To deal with the many sounds that fill the whale's world and from which it receives most of its sensory information, the acoustic center of a whale's brain is very well developed. The animal's auditory nerve is huge, and the association areas connected to its acoustic centers are folded to provide an abundant supply of nerve cells.

So sensitive are dolphins to sound that raindrops falling into their aquarium will cause them to leap into the air. At sea, they can dive deep enough to escape what to them must be an unbearable thumping sound, not the soothing pitter-patter we associate with rain.

The echoes they receive from their echolocation systems probably allow whales to create an image of their surroundings just as we form mental images from the images produced in our eyes. In fact, whales' images are quite likely more penetrating than ours. Their ultrasound waves pass through flesh and are reflected by internal tissue such as bone and air sacs. They "see" in much the same way that doctors use ultrasound to form a picture of a fetus within its mother's womb. A dolphin doesn't have to ask, "How are you?" Its sonar images provide all the information it needs to assess your health. Even burping the baby is easy for a mother dolphin. A sonar scan of the offspring's stomach reveals the gas bubble's position. A bump from mother in the proper place produces the desired burp.

Cetacean Communication

Odontocetes seem to use high-frequency clicks to detect ordinary objects in their path. To examine small objects in their vicinity carefully, they emit rapid-fire high-frequency clicks. But high-frequency clicks are not the only sounds made by whales. The moans, groans, and songs of the mysticetes as well as low-frequency sounds from odontocetes are also prevalent in the sea.

Dolphins appear to "shout" all the sounds that originated with land mammals—barks, squeals, squawks, and whistles.

Some cetologists believe that whales, particularly dolphins, have their own language, that they can talk with one another just as we do. Dr. John Lilly wants to use computers in an effort to analyze the sounds of dolphins with the hope of finding a way to communicate with them.

Dolphins can imitate human sounds by expelling air through their blowholes, but this doesn't mean they can communicate. Parrots, which are certainly not regarded as intelligent creatures, can mimic human sounds too.

Researchers in Hawaii have found that dolphins can learn to understand two- and three-word sentences, whether spoken or gestured. For instance, they can distinguish between the sentence, "Hoop, fetch, ball," which means find the hoop and carry it to the ball, and the sentence, "Ball, fetch, hoop"—find the ball and carry it to the hoop.

This probably means dolphins can learn that words stand for objects. However, it may be simply a conditioned response. Dogs, too, seem capable of responding to commands that are sentences, such as "Get the paper," or "Fetch the ball."

Many who have studied dolphins carefully claim their whistles are a means of communicating. A whistle of increasing frequency says, "Hey, here's something new, a stimulus that's not familiar."

A whistle of falling pitch signals distress or uncertainty, while a so-called double-humped whistle—one that twice rises and falls in pitch—indicates irritation.

Whistles of a pure tone seem to indicate, "I'm over here and my name is ——." Such whistles are common to dolphins in the sea as they herd fish for feeding. Such sounds may be a way of locating and identifying each other so that they will spread out properly as they chase fish in a systematic way.

Words are not our only means of communication. A "dirty look," a smile, a tear, or a shrug often communicates as much as or more than words. A dog's growl, raised hair along its back, or the position of its tail can warn us that the animal is not happy.

A dolphin seems to threaten another dolphin by facing it, mouth open, back arched. The other dolphin will often respond submissively by turning sideways with its mouth closed.

Dolphins also "talk" by touch as do all whales. The touching that seems so essential to the development of human infants and other primate young is clearly evident among whales. The mother whale maintains close contact with her young from birth. They are seen swimming side by side with flippers touching. "Naughty" youngsters are punished by a gentle slap with a flipper or by being pushed under or out of the water.

Smell is probably not used for communication among whales. The olfactory regions of their brains are miniscule or nonexistent, and their nostrils open only when they are out of water. However, they may well communicate by chemical stimuli in the water. Excretions and secretions of whales may leave a lingering taste in the water through which other whales swim. The diluting effect of the ocean is great, indeed, but eels somehow smell their way back to the Sargasso Sea, and small amounts of pheromones released by animals mark their territories or their sexual state. It may be that whales find their way across the seas by chemicals that they can taste.

It is evident that whales communicate with one another. Whether their system of communication is better developed than that of other animals is a question that future research will certainly try to answer.

Whaling: Giant-Killing at Sea

"... whether Leviathan can long
endure so wide a chase, and so
remorseless a havoc; whether he
must not at last be exterminated
from the waters."

As early as the ninth century Basque fishermen were killing right whales that swam along the coast of the Bay of Biscay. By the fourteenth century right whales were virtually nonexistent in the waters of Biscay. The profits they made selling whale oil for lamps throughout Europe led the Basques to kill right whales with little concern for the fact that the right whale population was finite. The profit motive and the demand for whale oil were so great that the Basques, after wiping out the herd in their part of the world, sent ships far out into the Atlantic in search of whales.

A Brief History of Whaling

Archaeological digs based on early Basque records discovered by Selma H. Barkham have revealed a sixteenth-century Basque whaling station on the coast of Labrador. These records show that as early as 1566, Captain de Cerain shipped one hundred harpoons and twenty-four lances to "Grand Bay."

Various pieces of evidence led Mrs. Barkham and others to believe that "Grand Bay" was the name of an inlet in Labrador that is now called Red Bay. Expeditions to this area, beginning in 1977, indicate that a whaling and cod-fishing community was indeed located in this area in the second half of the sixteenth century.

An abundance of whalebone along one beach area proved to be the remains of about thirty right whales, the species commonly pursued by Basque whalers. Nearby were stone walls blackened by what proved to be burnt animal fat, presumably left by the smoke from boiling blubber. In addition, evidence of a cooper's shop and his barrel staves were found as well as knives and harpoon points. A sunken ship, believed to be the *San Juan*, which was recorded as having sunk near shore in 1565, was discovered. Its hull was filled with the barrel staves and covers that probably once enclosed tons of whale oil.

By the eighteenth century the English, Dutch, and Danes had joined the Basques in pursuing and virtually eliminating right whales from the northeastern Atlantic Ocean.

The so-called golden age of whaling in America followed the Revolutionary War. By this time Yankee Whalers had harpooned most of the right whales along the coastal waters of the Northeast and were forced to pursue denser populations of whales in more distant waters.

Between 1804 and 1817 nearly 190,000 right whales were taken on whaling voyages to the South Atlantic. The southern New England ports of Nantucket, New Bedford, and Mystic became the whaling centers of the world. From 1820 to 1860 three-fourths of the whaling ships on the high seas flew the American flag. The demand for whale oil and whalebone enabled whaling companies and their captains to amass fortunes. Large vessels equipped with decks designed for flensing whales, and furnaces, caldrons, and barrels to boil blubber and store the oily product set out on voyages that lasted three or four years.

Though whaling companies reaped huge profits and stories made whaling sound adventurous and exciting, little money was made by the seamen who manned these dirty, stinking ships where the captain made the only laws. Seamen earned an average salary of twenty cents a day while living in cramped, damp, dank, dark, dirty quarters. Meanwhile, laborers ashore made four times as much and enjoyed far better food and living conditions. Only the myth of adventure on the sea and the willingness of whaling companies to hire the dregs of society led men to sign on whaling vessels. Life on board was so unpleasant that captains were reluctant to enter any port during a voyage for fear the men would desert.

A typical ship weighed 500 tons, required a crew of forty, and carried six 30-foot whaling boats that were used to chase whales when a sailor in the crow's nest shouted, "Thar she blows," or simply, "Blows."

Each boat, when in pursuit of a whale,

carried a coxswain who was an officer, four seamen, and a harpooner. Two seamen on the port side pulled long oars while two seamen and the harpooner on the starboard rowed with shorter oars. They approached a whale stealthily from in front or behind, for whalers knew that whales have a keen sense of hearing. One slap of an oar in an oarlock might put a whale into rapid motion or a deep dive.

At a signal from the officer, as the boat drew close to a whale, the harpooner would take up his position near the bow. His objective was to sink his harpoon into the whale as close to its eye as possible. When struck, the whale would usually swim away at high speed, trailing the long line attached to the harpoon. So fast did these animals move that the harpooner had to pour water on the line to keep it from burning.

Killing a whale was often a dangerous task.

As the whale pulled the small boat, now often far beyond sight of the mother ship, protocol required that the coxswain and harpooner walk the full length of the boat, high seas or not, and change places so that an *officer* might administer the coup de grace. This was done with a 5-foot spear that the coxswain plunged into the exhausted whale's head and then rotated.

At this point the whale was supposed to die, but, instead, it might attempt to bite the boat in half or slap at the craft with its mighty flukes. If the whale was killed, it then had to be towed back to the distant ship—a task that might require many hours of backbreaking rowing.

Clearly, whaling was a hard, dangerous occupation with little reward for those in the small boats.

Once the whale reached the ship, it was tied, tail forward, to the starboard side, where flensers cut away slabs of blubber that were thrown into caldrons and boiled down to oil amid a smoking stench that was nearly unbearable. If the animal was a sperm whale, the intestines would be opened to search for foul-smelling ambergris, which was highly valued when dried as a base for perfumes. The mouth of a mysticete would be stripped of its baleen and sold as whalebone. The remains of the whale were simply released into the sea where sharks that had been nibbling at the carcass during the flensing process would soon devour it.

In 1868 Svend Foyn's invention of the harpoon cannon changed the rules of the hunt for whalers. This gun often brought the swift-moving fin and blue whales within the harpooner's range. Now they, along with right, gray, sperm, and humpback whales, faced extinction. Within a decade, steam-powered ships enabled whalers to overtake the fastest of whales. The whales no longer had a chance. The challenge was gone. The hunt became a slaughter.

With the introduction of kerosene for lighting in the second half of the nineteenth century, the demand for whale oil declined. There was, however, a growing demand for whale oil's fine lubricating quality in the flourishing industries of this time, but the Civil War had destroyed the whaling fleet of the eastern United States.

Whalers, unaware of the war after a long voyage, were captured by privateers on their return from the southern hemisphere. And in 1861 forty whaling vessels loaded with rocks sailed from New Bedford, Massachusetts. They were sunk at the entrance to Charlestown harbor to prevent pirate ships and blockade-runners from leaving port.

An abundance of gray and sperm whales in the Pacific, together with the destruction of eastern whaling vessels during the Civil War, shifted America's whaling center from New England to San Francisco and Honolulu. A demand for the whalebone of baleen whales kept eastern whaling companies in business, but the golden age was over.

The early twentieth century saw a surge in whaling to meet the need for fine lubricating oil in industry and automobiles. Whale oil was also used in making soaps and paints, and in processing jute. Glycerin extracted from the oil was used for making explosives, but attempts to introduce whale meat in to the American diet after World War I were not successful.

The United States never made the transition to factory ships designed to capture, process, and store every part of a whale. A whaling boat associated with a factory ship will chase a whale until it tires, fire a harpoon that explodes shortly after it enters the whale's head, inflate the animal with air so that it will float, and mark it with a flag. Later the factory ship will arrive and drag the whale into its assembly line.

Every part of the whale is used for something. The development of hydrogenation in the early twentieth century allowed these floating factories to convert whale oil to margarine, candles, crayons, and cosmetics. The oil is also used in making varnish, ink, soap, and glycerin, as well as lubricants.

The meat, which has a stronger flavor than beef, is a delicacy in many Japanese restaurants and is an ingredient of that nation's school lunch program. The poorer cuts are used to make pet food. Bone within the meat is ground into bone meal and sold as an ingredient of animal food or as a fertilizer. Even the blood is made into a protein-rich powder.

Leather is made from the skin of toothed whales, and glue from the collagen in the animals' bones, skin, and tendons. The tendons can be used also for tennis racquet strings or surgical stitches. The teeth of odontocetes are used in making piano keys. Old-time whalers used them for making scrimshaw, decorative pieces that sailors carved during the boring hours on long voyages. The scrimshaw served as an article of trade in foreign ports.

An average whale liver can provide 5 to 7 pounds of vitamin A. The animal's glands are a source of ACTH and insulin, and ambergris is still sought from the intestines of sperm whales.

The baleen of mysticetes was once used for corset stays, hoops for skirts, umbrella ribs, whip handles, fishing rods, nets, and brushes. Today these baleen products have been replaced by steel and plastic. The same is true of other whale products. Even the prized spermaceti oil has been replaced with oil from the jojoba and crambe plants native to the deserts of North America.

As floating factories plied the Antarctic seas harvesting whales like giant thrashing machines, the world's whale population dropped dramatically. During the 1930–31 season alone, 40,201 whales were taken. Even whaling companies began to recognize a need for controls.

In 1937, at the London Convention, nine nations formulated the first international whaling agreement. They decided to protect the gray whale from further hunting, to limit the regions where factory ships might go, and to require a minimum length for each species of whale taken in a move to protect younger whales. In 1938 these same nations agreed to protect the humpback whale. The beginning of an effective whaling organization seemed to be evolving; however, World War II effectively ended whaling until 1945, as warring nations found other uses for whaling ships.

Following the war, in 1946, nineteen nations created the International Whaling Commission (IWC), which established seasons for whaling and forbade the killing of cow whales with calves and all young whales. It also established protection for right, gray, and humpback whales, which were near extinction, and established a natural preserve for whales from longitude 70° to 160° West.

Two IWC inspectors were placed on every factory ship and at every whaling station to see that regulations were enforced.

Quotas were established each year by the IWC, but the quotas were calculated on blue whale units (BWU). One BWU was equivalent to a catch of 1 blue whale, 2 fin whales, 2.5 humpbacks, or 6 sei whales. The quota for the first year was 16,000 BWU, but because there was no limit on any one species, whalers sought the giant blue whales because a single kill provided so much substance. Within a decade blue whales were so seldom seen that whalers began pursuing fin whales. Five years later fin whales were in short supply, and whalers were willing to settle for the more abundant but smaller sei whales.

By 1972 it was obvious that the BWU was not an effective unit for preserving the whale population because it set no quotas for individual species, some of which bordered on extinction. The IWC, in 1972, set quotas for each species on the basis of the maximum sustainable yield (MSY). The MSY is supposed to be the population level at which a species breeds most rapidly. Once a species reaches its MSY, according to the IWC, animals in excess of that number *should* be killed to keep the species reproducing at a maximum rate.

While this plan seemed satisfactory to whaling companies, it was not well received by many scientists who felt it was impossible to make accurate determinations of MSY for whales. We simply don't know enough about them. Furthermore, we cannot consider a species in isolation. Whaling may upset the ecological balance among species, or the ratios of the sexes and of young to old within a species.

Cuts in quotas imposed by the IWC seem to have been based, not on a difficult-to-obtain MSY, but on evidence from whalers that they could no longer take even the allowed quotas. The quota for 1976–77 for all species in the southern hemisphere was 20,000, but only 15,106 were taken. In 1956 sperm whaling peaked with a catch of 6,974 whales that provided 342,000 barrels of oil. In 1970 a catch of 3,090 sperm whales provided only 125,000 barrels. This decline of 20 percent in barrels of oil per whale indicates that smaller, younger whales are being killed, a trend that threatens the survival of the species.

A growing conservationist movement in the United States and other Western countries led members of Greenpeace to place themselves between Russian whalers and the whales they sought; it prompted pickets to shout outside IWC meetings; it caused the U.S. government to ban whaling product imports and to pass the 1972 Marine Mammal Protection Act; it led to the voluntary boycotting of Japanese and Russian goods by five million citizens until these nations cease whaling; and it sparked many other save-the-whale programs.

Whether in response to this movement or to a growing realization that the whale stocks were being depleted, IWC quotas steadily decreased from 46,000 in 1972–73, to 14,734 in 1981–82, and 11,331 in 1982–83.

Whaling Banned

On July 23, 1982, in Brighton, England, the IWC banned all commercial whaling for an indefinite period beginning in 1986.

Japan, Norway, the USSR, Brazil, Iceland, South Korea, and Peru voted against the ban.

Japan and the USSR each accounted for 39 percent of the world's recent take of whales. Norway's share was 12 percent. The remaining 10 percent is divided among Brazil, Chile, Peru, South Korea, and Spain. After the meeting, Spain announced that it is ending its small whaling industry. In Chile and Peru, whaling is operated largely by Japanese companies.

Sir Peter Scott, a British naturalist who is Great Britain's chief scientific adviser to his nation's IWC delegation, said, "This is the end of commercial whaling. . . . Now we must assess and take action to conserve other whales which come under the heading of aboriginal and subsistence whaling."

Scott's words may have been reassuring to Greenpeace members, but the IWC has no power to enforce its ban, though member nations may take punitive action against countries that continue taking whales after 1986. The United States, for example, has threatened to restrict the fishing rights of such nations within the 200-mile offshore area, and to prohibit fish imports from these countries. The Norwegians sell $50 million worth of fish products in the United States each year. Japanese fish exports to this country total $185 million a year, and the Japanese fish heavily in the coastal waters off the United States.

Norway, Japan, and the USSR have stated they will not agree to the ban.

The commission is to review the ban in 1990. If the whale population recovers in the four-year hiatus, the commission may reinstitute whaling and set new annual quotas. It is likely, however, that if whaling is disbanded for four years, it will never resume. Boats and men will not sit idly about for four years, particularly if the possibility that the whaling ban will continue is likely.

Japan will probably continue to send its whaling fleet to sea. The Japanese delegation to the IWC said the vote was an infringement of the rules adopted when the commission was established. The IWC's purpose was to safeguard both whales and the interests of the whaling nations. And Japan is still a whaling nation. For a number of reasons, it may continue to whale. It is an economic fact that the Japanese whaling industry employs 1,300 people, and, they claim, 60,000 in related industries. These people will be unemployed if whaling ceases.

A very different cultural, religious, and historical heritage creates a different attitude toward whaling in Japan. The Japanese view the IWC ban as American in origin, and they resent Americans imposing their view of whales and whaling on them.

"Why," they ask, "is it cruel to kill whales but not cruel to kill sheep, cattle, hogs, and poultry?"

When Chinese Buddhism was transferred to Japan in 702, meat was forbidden as food. Whale meat was considered fish, and so became a delicacy for which Buddhists developed a taste. Japanese still enjoy whale meat, but it is not readily available and cannot compete with meat now that McDonald's has found its way to Japan.

To the Japanese, America's attitude toward whales seems hypocritical. It was American whalers who harvested most of the whales from the waters around Japan in the nineteenth century. And it was Commodore Matthew Perry who visited Japan from 1852 to 1854 to open this secluded nation to the world and to establish refueling stations for whalers. Later, it was General Douglas MacArthur, after World War II, who encouraged Japan to resume whaling as one means of bolstering its postwar economy.

Political factors influence Japan's position on whaling, too. The coastal cities of Japan, where whaling companies are located, have a disproportionately strong voice in the national legislature. There is also strong pressure from labor unions and from the whaling industry, which has to pay severance bonuses to seamen who are laid off. The average bonus is $30,000. The end of whaling could cost these companies millions of dollars in severance pay alone.

Some conservationists fear that Japan's reaction to the ban may end the IWC and eliminate its growing strength as a force for conserving whales. It might be more effective in the long run to let Japan take a limited number of unthreatened whales and let the IWC concentrate on preserving the endangered species.

In an effort to persuade Japan to accept the moratorium on whaling, some conservationists have suggested that we:

1. Encourage Japan to promote the commercial potential of whale watching, a venture that has become a multimillion-dollar industry in the United States.
2. Increase the allowable catch of fish by Japanese in American waters as a way of compensating for the loss of the whaling industry.
3. End the hunting of bowhead whales by Alaskan Eskimos. (Since the bowhead is an endangered species and its extinction seems likely, the native culture built around this whale will soon end anyway.) Because whale meat is part of Japanese culture, the Japanese find it difficult to accept a whaling ban while another culture is allowed to continue whaling.

Whales and Morals

The reaction of Japan, Norway, and the USSR to the IWC ban on whaling raises the question of the morality of whaling.

Alaskan Eskimos are allowed to kill a certain number of bowheads—forty-five over three years—as a concession to their aboriginal culture, in which whaling is vital. These Eskimos hunt bowheads in light boats. Once they land a whale, these people, with flensing knives, can reduce an 8-ton bowhead to a spot on the ice between lunch and dinner.

Every part of the bowhead is used. The foot-thick blubber serves as fuel or as fox bait; the meat is stored in subterranean caches carved in the permafrost (a rather inexpensive deep freeze) where it serves as a food staple thoughout the year. Bowhead bones and baleen are used to make tools.

The innards are made into dog food. Mutuk, the skin together with a thin layer of blubber, is regarded as a delicacy when boiled and salted.

Of course, the number of whales killed by the Eskimos is small in comparison with the number that would be taken by the Japanese whaling fleet. But is the morality of killing whales related to numbers?

Those who make a moral case against whaling argue that:

1. The only nations opposed to the moratorium on whaling are those nations with whaling industries. This suggests that their real reason for opposing the ban are economic ones.
2. The aesthetic and educational value of live whales far outweighs the value of whale products, for which there are substitutes.
3. Unlike the slaughter of sheep, hogs, and cattle, where the animal dies instantly, several harpoons are often required to kill a whale, which may therefore suffer greatly before dying.
4. Every animal has a right to live, especially the whale, which does not harm humans, has a social structure, and seems to possess superior intelligence. There is so much we might learn from and about these animals that they should be preserved.
5. This generation has an obligation to preserve whales for the enjoyment and learning of future generations.

Whaling nations may argue that these moral arguments are the result of a particular cultural bias. To a Buddhist, taking an animal's life is abhorrent. Other cultures or religions forbid the eating of pork or cattle. Christians, however, have always viewed animals as something God created for human enjoyment and consumption. Matters of faith and culture are seldom based on reason, which makes a moral stand on whaling difficult to defend worldwide.

Certainly, a ban on whaling can be justified biologically in terms of the whale population, although methods of estimating the population of seagoing species give very different results. For example, estimates of the humpback population in the Pacific vary from 2,000 to 8,500. Since estimates of whale populations are not precise, it makes little sense to use MSY as a basis for IWC quotas, for we know neither the actual nor the MSY population.

Because we cannot isolate a species of whale from its ecological environment, how can we determine the consequences of eliminating a particular species of whale from the earth? Will other related species also become extinct? Or will one species reach unimagined levels because its natural predator is gone? Some believe the great right whale will never recover its numbers because sei whales have filled its niche. On the other hand, the gray whale may have recovered so rapidly because no other species took over its food and territory. Finally, cetaceans seem to form social groups. What is the effect of killing the dominant member of a family group? Are the other members then less able to survive?

There are so many unanswered questions concerning the biology of whales that it seems wise to err on the side of conservation, lest we lose these giants of the sea forever.

In his book, *The Blue Whale,* George L. Small makes a plea for conservation, though he fears the blue whale is a species that cannot be saved. Small writes:

The tragedy of the blue whale is the reflection of an even greater one, that of man himself. What is the nature of a species that knowingly and without good reason exterminates another? How long will man persist in the belief that he is master of this earth rather than one of its guests? When will he learn that he is but one form of life among countless thousands, each one of which is in some way related to and dependent on all others? How long can he survive if he does not? . . . Survival chances for the human race will be greatly enhanced when man concedes to the earth and all its life forms the right to exist that he wants for himself. The only homage he can now pay to the blue whale is to learn the lessons of dependence on and kinship with all life. If he does not learn them, the great blue whale will have died in vain—having taught nothing to his only mortal enemy.

From the whalers' viewpoint, a Japanese leaflet asked how Americans might feel if they were told they could not kill cattle. The leaflet went on to explain that the lack of land in Japan prevents that nation from growing beef. The Japanese must obtain their protein from the sea. The retort from the West is obvious: a farmer does not kill off his entire herd; he maintains his herd by breeding as many animals as he slaughters.

Farming methods may well offer a solution for these countries that believe whaling is essential to their economy and culture. More than fifteen years ago, Gifford Pinchot at Johns Hopkins University proposed using the Pacific coral atolls as "pastures" for whales. He suggested that windmills could provide energy to pump nutrients from the deep ocean water outside the atoll to the inside and thus increase the growth of plankton and zooplankton within the pasture. Baleen whales that feed on zooplankton could graze and breed within these giant atolls.

Whales could then be slaughtered in a controlled manner, at the same rate that new whales are born.

Whether whales, for whom migration seems a part of life, would survive and prove profitable to a whale farmer is an untested question. But if the Japanese really believe that whales are vital to their culture, they should be willing to run a pilot study to test Pinchot's idea. Since a growing blue whale can convert the krill it eats to 15 tons of meat in two years, whale farms might provide

Japan and other nations with all the whales they need without depleting wild stocks in the oceans. At the same time, scientists could study these marvelous animals at close range.

Whale farms are anathema to Western culture, but to the Japanese or Eskimos, whales are a source of food. They regard whales in the same way that we regard pigs, sheep, cattle, and poultry. We may disapprove of such farms, but their success could save the wild whales, which would no longer be hunted.

Bibliography

Burton, Robert. *The Life and Death of Whales*. New York: Universe Books, 1980.

Carriglar, Sally. *The Twilight Seas, A Blue Whale's Journey*. New York: Weybright & Tally, 1975.

Cousteau, Jacques-Yves, and Diole, Phillippe. *The Whale: Mighty Monarch of the Sea*. New York: Doubleday, 1972.

Ellis, Richard. *The Book of Whales*. New York: Alfred A. Knopf, 1981.

McIntyre, Joan. *Mind in the Waters*. New York: Scribner, 1974 (Sierra Club Books, San Francisco).

Scheffer, Victor B. *The Year of the Whale*. New York: Scribner, 1969.

Watson, Lyall. *Sea Guide to Whales of the World*. New York: Elsevier-Dutton, 1981.

The Whale. New York: Crescent, 1977.

INDEX

About the Author and Artist

Robert Gardner is head of the science department at Salisbury School, Salisbury, Connecticut, where he teaches physics, chemistry, and physical science. He did his undergraduate work at Wesleyan University and has graduate degrees from Trinity College and Wesleyan University. He has taught in a number of National Science Foundation teachers' institutes and is the author of several science books, including *Save That Energy; Water, The Life Sustaining Resource;* and *Kitchen Chemistry*. Mr. Gardner spent a sabbatical year at Columbia University doing independent study on a Klingenstein Fellowship he was awarded in 1983–84.

Don Sineti is a specialist in illustrating whales; he was the major illustrator of *Alaska Whales and Whaling*. Mr. Sineti is the founder and president of the Connecticut Cetacean Society and frequently leads whale watching trips on the East Coast.